Dream Big.
Hustle Hard.

The Millennial Woman's Guide to Success in Tech

Abadesi Osunsade

Dream Big. Hustle Hard.
The Millennial Woman's Guide to Success in Tech

Advice for graduates and 20-somethings.
Don't know what you want to do with your career?
Neither did I. With this book you will learn:

- How to use university to create experiences and get to know what you like in a job.

- How to land your first job in a startup - the perfect first job for curious, ambitious people.

- How to sell your strengths effectively to earn more and learn more than your peers.

- How to create your own standard of success based on your personal motivations (hint: your parents may not agree with it).

Table of Contents

Foreword by Jessica Rose

One of the greatest joys of my career has been my work helping to support people entering the technology industry. Resources like this book, which allow people to self serve valuable advice, have been an invaluable part of this work. I'm honoured to be introducing you to this, it's been designed to help millennial women approach and engage with work in technology from an informed position of power.

Perspectives from successful women in tech can be hard to come by and the lack of role models has a serious impact in the technology sector. Hearing from a successful woman of colour who broke into the industry without a computer science degree is even more rare and valuable. In this book Abadesi Osunsade pairs her industry experience with structured activities designed to prepare recent graduates and school leavers for work in technology. I would love to see young female technologists reading this book in groups and discussing the questions posed together. I have a rosy daydream of women gathering around this book to share their goals and bond with each other as they strike out into an often hostile industry.

I am a self-taught technologist focused on fostering equal access to work in technology. Through my work as a speaker, technical manager and in non-profits, I've been fortunate enough to see incredible women enter the industry and support each other. It is my highest hope that works like this will continue to enable the underrepresented to enter the industry to finally take what we deserve.

- Jessica Rose. Founder, Open Code and Co-Founder, Trans Code. Follow her @jesslynnrose

Foreword by Ryan Hoover

More than ever before, technology is shaping our culture, yet the tech industry – the people creating the apps and products we use every day – inadequately represents the makeup of its consumers. This book is one step to help change that, equipping young and motivated women to succeed in this field.

I grew up in Oregon, raised by two middle-class entrepreneurial parents. My father and mother have built and operated various businesses since I was a child. They encouraged me to pursue entrepreneurial projects, from managing gumball machines at 11 years old to reselling electronics on eBay in high school. They equipped me with strong work ethic and hoped that I too could eventually start my own business. And I eventually did.

I was born into fortunate circumstances but a job in tech was never given to me. I too had to work hard to make things happen. Regardless of your background, reading this book won't guarantee a successful career in tech. It's on you to apply these learnings and hustle.

-   Ryan Hoover. Founder, Product Hunt and Weekend Fund. Follow him @rrhoover

Dream Big. Hustle Hard.

Foreword by Claud Williams

I remember the walk back to my apartment after my last ever university exam. The sun was out, the air smelled like freedom and life seemed a little bit more beautiful. However, by the time I arrived home, my nagging thoughts had grown into a sense of dread as I began to realise that life was about to get real.

Today I run Dream Nation, a startup company with the mission to design a personal development brand for the 21st century. We've had the pleasure of working alongside amazing brands and individuals from companies such as Google, BuzzFeed, YouTube and more, however, getting to this point hasn't been easy.

I wish I had met someone like Abadesi earlier in my career. She has acquired a wealth of experience and wisdom from her career with organisations like the Financial Times, Groupon, Amazon and Product Hunt, while also building her own business, Hustle Crew.

In this book, Abadesi shares her insights, advice and wisdom in a step by step guide on how to create a successful career within the tech industry. You'll find a refreshing blend of personal stories, strategies and practical activities delivered in the relatable, enjoyable and easy to digest style Abadesi is famous for.

-    Claud Williams. Founder, Dream Nation. Follow him @claud_williams

Note from the Author

This book is intended to be read in a group, not alone at home. Why? Think of how many advice books you've bought with the best intentions but never actually finished or put into action. I can count at least a dozen on my bookshelves as I type this. When I read books with friends, I actually finish them. Together we push each other to get the most out of the content and stay accountable to our goals. I'm a part of a Lean In circle in London where we meet regularly to discuss Sheryl Sandberg's lessons and apply them to the challenges we are facing in our working lives. It's been an incredible way for me to learn and leverage not only the guidance in the book but the perspectives of other people. So if you're tucked up on the sofa at home alone ... stop. Pick up your nearest device and send a message to a few friends, friends who are up for a new challenge and always up for learning. Friends who are curious and ambitious and excited for what the future holds. Tell them you need a reading buddy to help you get through all the activities in "Dream Big. Hustle Hard". You can also join the community by following @hustlecrewlive on Instagram, Twitter and Facebook, where you can connect with other members of Hustle Crew and build your own reading squad. Now get to work! I would love to hear from you as you work through my advice in the book, email abadesi@hustlecrew.co.

PART I: MAPPING YOUR MOTIVATIONS AND CREATING YOUR PERSONAL STANDARD OF SUCCESS

Chapter 1
Starting out: What to do when you don't know what to do

- To know what you want to do for work, you need to understand what kinds of activities you find motivating.

- You can use a process of elimination to determine what you don't enjoy and be open to exploring what you might enjoy.

- Most career paths aren't a perfect straight-line people reach a happy place through trial and error - this is a good thing.

- We learn best from experience because experiences give us data points to make better informed decisions. You need data about yourself to make decisions about what kind of job you want to do.

How did I go from worrying that I would fail my degree to being headhunted by top tech companies like Amazon? Let's just say through a lot of hard work and trial and error, because I didn't have a master plan for my career. When I arrived at university, a bright-eyed fresher at the London School of Economics (LSE) in October 2006, I was overwhelmed by the abundance of fiercely intelligent people. I was studying a degree my parents were more passionate about than me, and really felt like an imposter. Don't get me wrong, I was excited to start my university studies, but being truly independent for the first time in my life was overwhelming. Like many obedient children of strict immigrant parents, I had spent so much of life being told what to do and obeying those commands, that being on my own for the first time left my mind free to wander and question things like my true motivations in education. It was a line of questioning that often made me feel confused about who I was and what I wanted out of life. I knew I wanted to be successful but I wasn't sure what that meant because my own opinions were so heavily influenced by my parents' ideas of success. Success for them was a job that brought you security, wealth and status. But would those three things alone make me feel fulfilled? I had my doubts.

My career and life, like everybody on this earth, has had its fair share of ups and downs since my fresher year. The adventurous road I've been on, combined with the extraordinary people I've met along the way, have made me realise there's no clearly defined path to success. And that's a good thing. It means anyone can draw their own path from where they are now to where they want to be in the future. Success is subjective. It's up to you as an individual to create your own standard of success to hold yourself accountable to. If you are willing to work hard for it and put yourself through some tough challenges, you can get there. You may not be the best in your field, but you'll be doing what you're passionate about. What's so great about status, anyway?

For me, making positive progress towards my career goals required a change in my limiting mindset, from thinking in binary, black and white terms - like right or wrong, succeed or fail, win or lose - to appreciating that the world is too complex to be simplified in this way. Success and failure are more like two ends of a spectrum than two sides of a coin. As I began to understand that these dichotomies I'd based my life decisions on were actually false, I began to be kinder to myself as I navigated through university life. I guess right and wrong could be a spectrum too? Or totally relative and subject to the specific situation, person, time or place. Perhaps it was time to revisit my life plan. I arrived at university assuming I'd get a good degree and land myself a job as a lawyer or economist at a reputable international organisation. In the checklist of my life, which my dad had drafted shortly after my birth with zero input from me, the post-university career step was already sketched out. Except, now that I was at university, that next step wasn't exciting anymore. Now I found myself at LSE, it was as if the curtain had lifted and I realised there were thousands more career opportunities available to me. I was overwhelmed by the choices and feeling pressured by the responsibility of having to choose The Right One. My old way of thinking, the framework I used to make decisions, just didn't seem to work anymore. It seemed limiting and one-dimensional. How could I start to undo a lifetime of limiting behaviour and allow myself the freedom to make bolder choices?

I grew up in a strict patriarchal household where my parents, my Nigerian dad particularly, put a lot of pressure on me to always get the top grades. For him, the world of education was very black and white - the main purpose of education was to secure top grades in order to land a spot at a renowned university and then a well-paid job at a reputable institution. Because of my dad's obsession with education and good grades, from a young age I began to obsess about achievement and perfection. I knew that to succeed at school, I had to listen to my teachers, work hard and get the highest grades. Surely I could just do this forever - obey the commands of my superiors - and things would work out, right? I did not anticipate that life after school would be full of so many decisions and that professors would not really give you life advice in the same way teachers did.

My narrow view of achievement didn't help me when I got to LSE. I assumed that I could just carry on as I had done throughout all my life, follow the syllabus to a tee, work hard, listen to my teachers and things would eventually fall into place around me - the right job, the right career. Except the careers world isn't like school. There's no clear step-by-step process. Unless you're studying a vocational degree that leads to a specific profession, there is no obvious next step post graduation. I studied Economics and Government and like many geeky social scientists, studying the theories seemed more thrilling than applying them to real life. Where was the Idiot's Guide to Building a Successful Career that I so desperately needed? It was clear to me that in the job market, there are no rules and regulations decreeing what should be on a syllabus or at what age one should be ready to graduate. It's not a consistent ecosystem set up to support and guide you, like schools. The career world is a dynamic ecosystem that's constantly changing, a world where your time and labour become resources that corporations want. In the careers world you are not only a person - you are a commodity. A necessary ingredient for a company to operate. This means you are investing your life, your youth, your abilities and your ideas into making a company   successful.

There has been more transparency about the career world in recent years, thanks to social media and countless online resources, workers have become more clued-up about the opportunity cost of working in an office and so corporations have started investing more in the employee experience - personal development, skills training, and perks. But that doesn't change the fact that you give your best energy and ideas to the organisation you work with. You spend more time doing your job than hanging out with your friends, your family and pursuing your hobbies. And since that's the case - shouldn't you pick wisely? Another shift that has occurred for kids of the 90s and beyond - for better or for worse - is the link between our careers and identity. I feel that more so than my parents, my job is a reflection of me. It is a core part of my identity. I can't clock in, clock out, and stop thinking about work once I leave. What I do is a reflection of who I am, it's not something I can hide from my friends or others who I care about. It's something I want to be proud of, something I can get excited talking about. No pressure then!

So how do we decide what to do after graduation? Most of us have little or no real life work experience by the time we get to university. That's why it's helpful to use university opportunities to better understand our likes and dislikes. Through participation in sports teams and student societies, we have a chance to immerse ourselves in new experiences. Gaining new responsibilities allows us to flex our skills and learn about ourselves - is this role exciting? Challenging? Frustrating? While you're studying, you can take up a leadership position as a committee member, or even run for an elected position governing your student body. As you approach these challenges think about what skills you need to succeed. These are the skills you will be developing in the role. For example, if you decide to be Treasurer for your university's Women in Business society - you will need to have strong numerical skills and be able to balance a budget. If you take up a position as a reporter for your student newspaper, you will need strong communication skills and storytelling abilities. If you join the debating team, you will develop your public speaking skills. What skills and abilities do you enjoy using? Which ones do you have a natural flair for? Take notes, as these skills will help you decide what jobs to apply for, what jobs you might enjoy.

Through creating new experiences you begin to gather empirical data about yourself. And as any good student knows, data enables us to make well-informed decisions. This is why people read dozens of online reviews before deciding which new laptop to buy, or which hotel to book for their vacation. But most schooling doesn't give us the opportunity to gather career-related data about ourselves. It's why so many of us struggle to decide what to do after university. We also feel pressured into making the right choice - it feels as though the remainder of our lives, whether it be happy or sad, a failure or success, hinges on making the right choice. I used to think that, and now I know that's not true.

Dream Big. Hustle Hard.

By the time I got to final year, I still wasn't sure what my career would be. I felt lost - there were a number of possibilities. But which one was right? Which one would make me most successful? Rich? Happy? Like most confused soon-to-be-graduates I turned to my parents again. My dad wanted me to be an economist but at LSE my confidence in my quantitative skills had been completely destroyed. I would spend hours on problem sets that more skilled mathematicians in my class could solve in minutes. Was I really considering a career where I would always feel like 'the dumb one'? The truth was that econometrics, a necessary skill, was a turn-off. I didn't fancy the idea of spending my life in a career where I was always playing catch up to peers who were passionate about number-crunching. I wanted to hone in on my natural abilities and maximise them to their potential. There were so many things other than maths that I really enjoyed and excelled in.

My stepmom wanted me to be a lawyer. And to be fair I did love watching law dramas on TV, not that they are a true reflection of the profession, but your interest has to be piqued somehow. She used to say, "You're so good at arguing and debating, you'd be great as a lawyer and you'd earn so much money". She always made a convincing case for it, and I thought it would be irrational to rule it out without some actual real life experience. A part of me suspected I'd find it too stuffy and boring but wanted to show my parents I was taking their advice seriously and exploring the opportunity.

So I found myself applying for an advocacy competition with a prestigious firm in the City in the summer of my second year. The winners would receive cash prizes as well as an interview for a place on their internship scheme. I figured, 'let's see if the law is for me', even though a part of me really couldn't picture myself wearing black suits all day poring over briefs and being bossed around by stiff-lipped partners. With the help of a friend who was studying a law degree, I researched and rehearsed my application speech,

Dream Big. Hustle Hard.

Working as a sales associate in Selfridges during university made me realise that I had a knack for sales. My impression of sales was quite basic before I started the job. I had images in my mind of media stereotypes - a door to door salesman from the 1950s, cold calling sales operators in dingy boiler rooms, or under-appreciated perfume ladies on shop floors. Little did I realise how valuable a sales team is to a business, and how many different types of sales roles there are. Most importantly, I soon realised sales was more than just about making a sale; it was really about connecting with people, something I had a natural flair for. Suddenly I was leveraging the skills that came naturally to me - talking to people, being inquisitive and friendly, finding out about them - and using the details I learned to my advantage, to better serve the customer needs. All this for a decent wage. Through my job I not only learned about my working abilities but also my preferred working conditions. I began to understand the merits of a desk-based job after getting sore feet from standing on the shop floor all day. Through working with a real mix of people - some extrovert, some introvert, some intellectual, some completely fashion obsessed - I began to understand more about the types of co-workers I felt most positive around and therefore the kind of company cultures I would gravitate towards. Think about what jobs are within your reach, and how they can help you understand yourself in the workplace better.

When I told my friends that my ordeal of interviewing for a vac scheme left me feeling like a lawyer's life was not for me, they said I was silly for giving up on the law so quickly "Do you know how much money you can earn once you're qualified? Imagine being on six figures before you're 30." they said. But I had to trust my gut and what felt right to me. I knew in my heart it wasn't my calling because I felt it instinctively that I was not motivated by money or by prestige and I wanted to do something where I could be more creative. I only applied for the competition because of pressure from my parents. My heart wasn't in it. Being rich wasn't an accomplishment that was calling out to me. I had no interest in doing things like wearing designer clothes and dining at Nobu every week just because I could afford it. I also knew that with that pay cheque came a bigger sacrifice - my time. The corporate lawyers that I knew, LSE graduates a few years above me, worked until the early hours of the morning. They rarely did social stuff mid-week like going to exercise classes, meeting with friends or going on dates. They had no work-life balance. It wasn't for me. Spending quality time with those close to me has always made me happy and I wanted that to be a big feature in my life. I didn't want a job where there would always be an expectation that work / the client came first.

We spend most of our waking lives at work - are we really just chasing a label? "Rich" "Successful" "Accomplished"? Are we pursuing a parent's vision of our lives, a vision we may not fully subscribe to? What about our own personal fulfilment? I think as individuals we need to approach the job hunt more rationally. To be successful in any role you need to be motivated by the work, and to be motivated by the work you need to understand what the work involves and what is required of you to do it. This level of understanding requires real-life experience and interactions with people already in the role.

Activity:
- Make a list of all the jobs you've had since you were in your early teens (it doesn't have to be an official salaried job, it could be a volunteering position, work experience or a summer camp)

- For each position you've held, list the aspects you liked most (e.g. inputting data into Excel), and which you liked least (e.g. interacting with customers)

- Using this list, what themes can you develop about the types of things you enjoy at work and the types of things you don't enjoy at work?

- Think of the skills you used in these roles e.g. organisational skills, communication skills.

Framework:

Use the data you've collected to make a list of your personal career priorities, the three top things you want out of a job e.g. lots of money, new skills training, international travel. Now as you approach the job hunt, make a list of all the roles that interest you. I like to use a Google Sheet / Excel to build a table that has all the key information I need as a column heading: Company, Job Title, Job Link, Application Due Date, etc. Use your priorities to create a ranking system that helps you sort out all the job opportunities in order of preference. It might be that your priorities change over time or as you start investigating different roles. That's to be expected. But stay focused on three key things which really matter to you. This will help you pick which roles amongst the thousands available out there would be most fulfilling to you right now.

tl;dr

- Use work experience and part-time jobs to better understand yourself in the workplace and form ideas of what could be a rewarding graduate job.

- The job market is ever-changing, dynamic, and your time is a valuable resource to employers so choose a role wisely, taking into account your career priorities.

- Create your own standard of success if you really want to find fulfilling work. Your parents' advice is framed by their own experiences of life and therefore may not be relevant for your life.

Chapter 2
Priorities: How to make time to get stuff done

- To be more productive you need to gain a better understanding of the conditions under which you work best.

- You need to reflect on what's worked and what hasn't and devise a strategy that helps you succeed, knowing what you know about yourself, warts and all.

- You should share your goals with someone you can trust who can help you stay accountable and not fall into bad habits.

Time management is something we all struggle with, but when you get it right, it can feel like you've gained an extra hour in the day. I spent all of secondary school struggling to balance all my work and subjects. I was prone to procrastination and distraction, but always put pressure on myself to do my best and deliver the highest standard of work I could. This resulted in many late night essay writing sessions, fuelled by the healthy balanced diet of Diet Coke and Haribo. During A levels I got into the habit of doing all my philosophy essays this way. Typically, the night before they were due was also the night the latest episode of The OC aired. It meant all of us girls would gather in the common room (I went to an all girls boarding school - traditional parents, what did you expect?) where it was the TV event of the week if not the main event of the week.

Dream Big. Hustle Hard.

When the theme song came on, like a chorus we would all sing, 'CALIFORNIAAAAA here we cooooooome'. There was no way I could miss an episode, the room would be packed and everyone would be there. This was before everyone had Netflix where you can have every TV dream on demand. Once the episode ended, I would hit up the vending machine for some sweets and soda. I'd head back to my room, flick the lamp on my desk and sit down to write. Books open around me, I'd begin writing my essay. I would always hand write them meticulously with a fountain pen. It wasn't very common to type your essays back in 2005/2006. I don't think students hand write four page essays anymore. Needless to say this wasn't the most effective studying system.

When I got to university, my workload increased a lot, as did my free time, freedom and partying. I realised my old way of meeting deadlines was unsustainable. I started trying to be more organised and disciplined with my time. It helped that most LSE students were incredibly studious. On any given day the library would be rammed full of students diligently getting through readings, problem sets, and chatting. Mostly moaning about how much work they had to do. I look back at that time and sometimes wonder if I would have got more done if I had spent less time talking about how much I had to do?

I read articles online about how to be organised and looked to the students who got the best grades and who I admired. I noticed many of them had a routine. In addition to our set timetables, they would carve out set times to work on assignments and readings. I decided to do the same, doing my best to stick to the schedule and ensure I was getting my work done consistently and steadily. Not leaving it all to the end and rushing in a frantic hurry. It was an incredible discovery. Even though it was hard to stick to it at first - and trust me, I didn't always stick to it - when I did get in the rhythm I found myself more focused than usual. It was easier for me to prioritise my work and actually get through

14

it.

I started socialising with my classmates more, particularly in the courses which I found most challenging. I would chat to my classmates who had received distinctions in their assignments, and ask if I could work through the next assignment with them or, in exchange for a coffee and cake, get their help with a tricky topic I couldn't wrap my head around. I realised they were often better at explaining the more complex stuff than my professors. Across my subjects I befriended the straight A students. Typically they were introverts, and as an extrovert, I may have come across a bit intense or a bit too much at first. But as time went on we became study buddies. I provided the jokes, coffee and snacks, while they provided the extremely helpful explanations and the genius.

I found it hard to ask questions in lectures and in class at LSE. The average level of intellect in the room was overwhelming. Despite being an academic scholar at my school, and a straight A student, being surrounded by other high achievers made my confidence shrink. When you're in such a big group, full of incredibly intelligent people, with a professor who is at the top of his field explaining something to you - it takes guts to acknowledge you didn't quite grasp the concept. It's intimidating. Particularly for women in my view. We live in a world that makes us strive for perfection and so fear failure more than other, more rational threats. Instead of putting my hand up and exposing my ignorance, I would scribble down my notes and remember to ask someone to explain it to me afterwards. Someone bright enough to get it the first time round.

Top tip: Include peers that you admire in your social circle, it's a great way to spur yourself to push further than you might otherwise. They will be a source of inspiration and will also share insights and advice that you can leverage.

Dream Big. Hustle Hard.

The transition from ambitious high school student to ambitious uni student is a tough one, especially if you secure a place at a competitive university. Competitive universities are full of exceptional students from across the country and the globe. I went to a small private all-girls boarding school called Roedean with about 300 students in total, aged 11-18. As a scholar and prefect I was used to getting the top grades and straight A's and suddenly at university… I was struggling! This was something totally new to me, I couldn't believe that no matter how many times I read a text or stared at a problem, I still couldn't make sense of it. I was in over my head. Worse still, having not done maths A-level, which subsequently became a compulsory requirement for my degree, meant that I was diving into the deep end in all my quant courses.

I couldn't do any of my micro-economics problem sets on my own, I always had to be with a group who had done maths A-level and who could walk me through the complex calculus and algebra that I had never learnt. Thankfully I hadn't lost my ability to write a good essay, so I was getting firsts in my government courses and loving every minute of it. But I knew, that for the first time in a long time, I needed a new approach to studying so I could stay at the top of my game.

I realised that it didn't make sense to give equal time to all my four courses when I was suffering so disastrously in two of them. I decided to be more structured in my time management, and allocate studying time based on which subject needed the most improvement. Because my essay subjects - political theory and governance - were relatively easy to me (I devoured the readings because I was engrossed in the subject and had strong opinions about the academics' interpretations) I could spend less time on them than on maths and economics.

I would start each day with the hardest subjects because that's when I felt my brain operated at its peak and greatest efficiency - it was fresh and clear after a good night's sleep and primed for concentration and unwavering focus. Even though I was tempted to start work on my essays because I loved writing and it came naturally to me, I knew that wasn't a smart move. I wanted to indulge my passion (and maybe my ego, too, just a little bit) and read and write and read and write. But I thought again about time management best practices - and how most efficiently I could spend my time. I realised I could easily fall into the distraction of writing, reading, and internet surfing. When really I should be channelling that peak mental energy into the work that needed my attention most. These were my maths and econ subjects where I was regularly getting marks in the 40 percent range - I had never got anything below 80s in my life as far as I could remember.

Now I know always to prioritise the hard things first. It's important for you to find out when your brain is at its peak and work on the hardest assignments you have then. Divide your day into units of time and think of what proportion you need to allocate to your different activities, remembering that the more challenging activities should have more time devoted to them than the easier ones. Impulsively it's easy to give the most time to what we enjoy, but to develop and grow we need to give adequate time to the areas that need development. Even if the challenging part of the activity puts us off.

Activity:
- Think about your daily routine - what time of day does your brain operate at its best?

- Are you planning your work so that you're working on projects during this time? If not, why not?

- Are there obstacles holding you back from working when your brain is most efficient? List the obstacles. Circle the ones which you can control. Write down a solution to clear that obstacle from your path.

- Enlist the help of friends or family to help you stay accountable to your new timetable and your work schedule goals.

- Can you create incentives to help you stick to your efficient schedule? E.g. if you do the work you need to do as planned, treat yourself to something you enjoy.

Framework:
When you have a big assignment or project, estimate how many hours of your time it will take to complete the project. Be as realistic as possible - consider all the stages and the corresponding time e.g. planning, researching, writing, etc. Break the project down into each part and assign a corresponding time you think it will take to complete that task. Once you have the total units of time in hours e.g. 35 hours, open your calendar and block out units of time to work on the project between now and its deadline. If there's no set deadline, set one for yourself to create accountability and minimise procrastination. Think back to previous similar projects you've worked on and decide if you work best in short bursts or big blocks of time. Block out the times in your calendar accordingly. Consider setting reminders so that when the time to work on your project begins - you stop everything you're doing and begin the task. Again, create accountability partners from your personal network - a partner, a parent or a friend who can check in on your progress at regular intervals, e.g. a weekly WhatsApp.

tl;dr
- Learn what time of day your brain works best, based on the time when hard work is easier to do and do your most challenging work in that time to maximise your productivity.

- Befriend the most accomplished students at your university and copy their best practices so that you too can be great like them.

- Work on breaking your bad habits now - procrastinating, all-nighters, sugar rushes followed by insulin comas - or they will haunt you for the rest of your life.

Chapter 3
How to secure your 'perfect' first job after university

- Your perfect first job will be the one that exposes you to as many different functions of the business as possible.

- Gaining experience is key as you are still at the start of your career and don't know enough about yourself or the job market to know what will make you feel fulfilled.

- Working in a startup enabled me to understand through close collaboration how different departments work and how businesses work.

- The internet is a powerful resource: research roles, companies and industries online to gain a better understanding of what it's like to work in them.

The astute observers amongst you will probably have guessed that this title is a misnomer. There is no perfect job, in fact there are dozens if not hundreds of possible jobs that you might enjoy doing and excel in. Really! Many of the university students I speak to at careers events and through coaching sessions often have the same desires when it comes to what to do after university. They tell me they want to be lawyers, strategy consultants or investment bankers. My heart always sinks when I hear this because it makes me realise how little university has changed in the ten years since I was a fresher.

At LSE I often felt like we students were on a conveyor belt. It was as if our institution was in cahoots with all the big corporates in London, as if some secret agreement had been made somewhere down the line that LSE would work us hard, stretch our brains and convince us of the merits of joining the City, so we'd be ready and willing to be the latest intake at the top banks and firms. Careers fairs on campus were often dominated by the same brands. The big corporates, the big banks, the big firms. So I am not surprised when students tell me their aspirations. It's all they see and all they are told to do. Between studying and socialising there's little time to explore other options beyond what is shown to you by your careers department. But if you're reading this book I suspect it's because you're already aware of the different possibilities available to you, which may not be as well advertised but certainly exist. In the UK, digital technology is the fastest growing sector in the economy, creating nearly 3 million new jobs between 2016 and 2020. Unfortunately, digital technology companies don't have the same presence on campus as bigger corporates, so students don't realise there are incredible opportunities to make an impact, develop and learn at these organisations, with no need to be a 'techie' or know how to code.

One of the best decisions I made during university was taking up my part-time job working as a retail assistant in Selfridges. I did a weekday evening and full day weekend shift each week and it was a great way to make some extra money, especially as I could earn commission on all my sales. As I mentioned before, I'd never actually done a proper retail sales job before this one, but in the job description retail experience was a requirement. So like many of us just starting out in the working world - I embellished the truth. During previous summer vacations I had dabbled in various work experience assignments so, on my CV to Reiss, I made these work experience stints appear more sales-oriented than I felt they were. It worked. After an interview in Head Office where I talked my way through a few real life (but not so real life) examples, I got the job.

I really enjoyed it. Not only did I get to work with lots of cool, interesting people (most of whom were fashion students and stylists), and serve celebs (like James Corden who once popped in with his partner), I also realised through the job that I was pretty decent at sales. Most weeks I would earn a decent commission of a few hundred pounds on top of my normal wages. And all this just by chatting with customers, answering their questions or helping them put an outfit together for a big occasion. As someone who started reading Vogue when I was 10 and was generally pretty clued up on fashion, it was fun helping out the less fashion confident to put different colours and styles together - watching their smiles grow as they realised they looked great in an outfit they wouldn't have necessarily picked out for themselves. Why did no one tell me sooner you could get paid just to chat with people and play dress up?

This experience made me realise that whatever job I did after university, I wanted to make building relationships and interacting with new people a key part of it. I wished there was a job where I could be exposed to all the different departments of an organisation. Like the shop floor, I craved an environment with minimal hierarchy, where everyone was open, friendly and able to be themselves. I wanted to immerse myself in more experiences and environments to continue building the mental image of what my ideal job would look like. I started applying to graduate schemes where you can rotate around different departments - these were grad schemes at marketing and advertising agencies. Having decided the law and banking were too stuffy I figured a more creative industry might suit me better.

Again, as I went through the recruitment process and started meeting people from marketing and advertising agencies, I realised my assumptions were wrong. Many of the recruiters I met were like all the other cookie cutter corporate types. Showing up to one of the assessment days, I was expecting to come face to face with quirky hipsters, modern day Don Drapers. Instead I saw, again, a bunch of middle aged white men in suits. Not quite the colourful and creative environment I was expecting. I went back to the drawing board. Turning over all the experiences I had gathered at university I tried to make an informed decision about what would be an enjoyable job. My list of what I would not enjoy was a lot longer than my list of what I would enjoy. One thing stood out as something I had always found exciting, motivating and interesting - writing for my student newspaper. And so I applied for an editorial internship at the Financial Times and successfully gained a place. I thought, "What a relief, my life is finally sorted". I was wrong.

Once again I found myself immersed in a new working environment. The day started with editorial meetings with the Editor-in-Chief, Lionel Barber. I found them really exciting. As an intern I stood at the back in awed silence, as the various Editors sitting at the round table would pitch their leading story and wait for feedback. It was so exciting to be behind the scenes of a newspaper I'd admired when I was growing up, and seen tucked under the arms of busy and important looking people on the tube. As an intern, I was rotating around different desks, starting with Technology. A new smartphone had been released dubbed 'the iPhone killer' and I set off with my mentor, a senior reporter, to the press event. After taking some notes and quotes we headed back to the office to prepare our write up and a few hours later it was published on FT.com. I had my first by-line and it felt great.

I started thinking, "Yeah - I could live this life, I could do this". Until my next assignment. The next day I was scanning the wires - a system with a live feed of all the latest stories breaking around the world. Hoping I might get the chance to sink my teeth into something juicy, my mentor approached me with an assignment. The government had just announced a new white paper which, if it became law, would negatively affect the pensions of elderly citizens. An editor wanted me to do some 'vox popping'. When the words left his mouth I had no idea what vox popping was. Thankfully there's Google. It's Latin for 'voice of the people' when journalists hit the streets to get commentary and insight directly from the public. Since this news would affect pensioners, I had to find some. But the editor had already thought this through - there was a constituency with one of the highest numbers of pensioners in the UK located a two hour train journey away. Next thing I know I'm on a train to Dorset, and after that, wandering the high street with a dictaphone asking pensioners to give me their opinions for my article. It wasn't easy. I spent the first half hour timidly wandering the high street seeking out a friendly face. There weren't many. I also noticed the lack of other non-white faces as I walked through the town centre. I hoped this wasn't working against me. Finally, as I was almost giving up hope, I stumbled upon a group of friends - retired Post Office workers and civil servants - playing chess on a bench and interviewed them all. I caught a train back to London and wrote my article.

A couple of months into my internship something dawned on me - the realisation that while I really enjoyed the process of writing, I didn't really enjoy the process of being a journalist. It seemed as though journalists had to do a lot of campaigning, which didn't appeal to me. Campaigning to the Editor-in-Chief to get your story on the front page of your section, campaigning with people in the industry to give you an exclusive scoop, even campaigning with strangers on the street to get that perfect soundbite. It was also around this time that the world in general started talking about the future of print - with online news being the default source for many people. The future of printed newspapers like the FT didn't look bright. Another mentor who managed me on my internship quite bluntly said - "Don't start your career in an industry that's dying". So I figured this wasn't quite what I thought it would be.

The nail in the coffin of my journalist career aspirations came late one Friday evening towards the end of my internship. I was preparing a report for the Markets section which required me to pull data from a Bloomberg Terminal, round up the decimal places according to the format required, and re-format the data into the tables published every week in FT Weekend. I was dealing with completely new systems for this assignment and felt totally overwhelmed. A senior reporter who was supposed to help me got caught up in a story he was chasing, so I tackled the task along despite not being entirely sure what I was doing. In hindsight, I should have asked someone with more experience to check my work as I was doing it. But I didn't. So I completed all the graphs required, totally wrong. Needless to say the Editor was not pleased, he blasted me for getting it wrong and the minute he stopped I retreated, straight to the women's toilet where I cried in a cubicle. "You idiot" I chanted to myself. I may not have wanted the job, but now I knew I wouldn't get an offer. After a quick 'get it together' session I returned to my desk where the senior reporter was back to very kindly to help me redo every graph. It was 9pm before I got home that night but phew was I relieved that it was the weekend. I had two days to build up the courage to face the Editor again. And of course, come Monday, it was like nothing even happened. Just another day in the newsroom.

It was only when I started working in a startup that I realised there might be something close to the perfect job after university. I joined Groupon in the spring of 2011, 18 months after graduating. The job I fell into after the FT just wasn't cutting it. I was producing conferences for investment bankers and corporate chief financial officers in glamorous cities like Rio de Janeiro and Dubai. It had great travel perks, but it was literally a job I fell into. Autumn 2009 wasn't a great time for the graduate job market thanks to the financial crisis and subsequent global recession. So after my FT internship I was desperate. Some of the best students I knew at university were still job hunting. I was worried. I gave my CV to every recruitment agency I could find and finally received an offer for a role I found interesting and well paid enough to take on. But I always felt like it was a stop gap for me - something to do until the economy improved and I found something more suited to my interests and skills.

By the time I joined Groupon there were already a lot of friendly faces from university working there. Knowing first hand their positive experiences of the company made me more confident in pursuing the opportunity, but it still felt a bit crazy. I had just left a safe and secure job in the City to come to work for a startup that had no guarantee of even existing in a few years' time. Of course my parents weren't best pleased. To make it worse, I was taking a pay cut, as all new employees had to start on a trial internship, which would be converted into a better paid full-time role if you performed well. Something just felt right about this opportunity. Everyone that I had spoken to or interacted with during the recruitment process had that spark that I always felt missing from the more corporate companies. There was a tangible energy and excitement Groupon employees gave off and it was contagious. I wanted to be a part of it.

On my first day I realised what it means to work at a real startup. These days every young up-and-coming company goes by the name, but Groupon's London office in 2011 really was. The company was growing at a pace no one could have planned for. To the point where we didn't even have enough seats or desks in the Partner Management department - the team I was joining. It had recently been created to handle all merchant related operations for the daily deals site. We fostered the relationships with the merchants once their sales representative had agreed the terms of the deal, and ensured that the design and editorial were all to their liking. I was told I'd be working on deals in Ireland and squeezed up in the only free space I could find, a patch of desk with a folding chair.

All around me the office was abuzz, phones were ringing, sales pitches were unfolding, fierce debates would blaze as raucous laughter ripped off in the background. I had never found myself in an environment like this before. And I loved it. I was struck by how much everyone seemed to be acting so natural, like themselves. There was no stuffiness. There was a lot of diversity. Posh people. Ordinary people. White people, black people, Asian people, mixed race people. Every combination you could think of. There were hijabis laughing next to super hip looking guys and super jock looking guys. There were people with pink hair and blue hair. It was incredible. As my laptop home screen was loading I turned to the guy next to me and introduced myself. "Hi, I'm Aba. I'm a new Partner Manager." Turns out he created the Partner Management department and back in The States sat next to the founder, Andrew Mason. Yet here he was, squeezed between me and another newbie, just doing his thing. No Big Deal.

Having worked in hierarchical environments it was refreshing to have such a flat structure. It was also refreshing to have so much freedom and autonomy when it came to solving problems. At this point we didn't have systems - no CRM like Salesforce, no sophisticated databases. It was scrappy. But from the scrappiness came invention and creative problem-solving. I would often ask our Department Head, Richard, what to do about x,y,z, to which he would often respond, "What do you think we should do?" At first, it confused me. I worried it might be a trick question like he might be trying to catch me out. But he explained that he was open to trying new things to see which solution would be most effective, most efficient.

In other words, he was genuinely curious about what I thought could be a fix. And that's how we got stuff done in those early days. We were all tinkerers, builders and inventors. Working cross-functionally with departments like Finance and Customer Services, we would tackle our merchants' and customers' problems head on and work towards mutually beneficial solutions. Through this scrappy startup way of working I was able to understand what my colleagues in other departments do on a day-to-day basis. It was eye-opening. It was great to learn about what it's like to be a designer, an in-house lawyer, or back-end engineer.

I can't think of any environment other than startups which let you work so intimately with all the departments in an organisation. Working closely with other teams, and immersing yourself in their work enables you to understand what that job is like and whether it is something you would like to do. In the early days of Groupon my colleagues moved departments all the time. After a few months on one team they would realise they were more interested in a totally different part of the business. We were still so informal and growing so fast that it was perfectly manageable for somebody to move into a new team, or even create a hybrid role. There was always a lot to get done, the leadership team wasn't too concerned with how things got done or who did them, we just needed to keep the customers happy.

This attitude changes as a company matures and grows, because with maturity comes bureaucracy - the rules and regulations that keep a big machine like a corporation running smoothly. Joining a grad scheme for a company that employs tens of thousands of people globally, even if it has rotations, won't let you learn in the hands-on way of a startup. And it won't let you really experience the different teams and different functions in a way that helps you understand yourself better. In a way that helps you realise what you find interesting, what you find motivating and what you would most enjoy in a job.

Activity:

- It's difficult to think objectively about ourselves. Only through self-reflection can we improve our self-awareness and start making better informed decisions.

- Spend some time doing some introspection. Create a document - it can be prose, a spreadsheet or even just use your notebook.

- Think about projects you have worked on, on your own and in a team. List down the things you liked and disliked about each experience.

- Think about the things you found really challenging in these experiences, channel any negative emotions you felt. Why was the experience challenging? What is the source of the negative memories?

- Can you learn anything about yourself and how you behave in certain situations, that could help you in the future?

- Can you learn anything about yourself, and the conditions under which you thrive vs conditions under which you are stressed?

- What elements of the project did you most enjoy? Maybe you're a fan of qualitative research, or perhaps you prefer more quantitative analysis.

Remember that your motivations are likely to change over time and that's OK. In this activity you're not aiming to find an answer that will sort you for life. You're aiming to find an answer that will sort you for the next chapter in your life.

Framework:
This is a prioritisation framework which, similar to a decision tree, helps you make objective decisions between roles which might be difficult to compare at face value. Rank your motivations / priorities from the last the chapter's activity in order of preference and importance. Now think about which two matter most to you and why. Now sketch a graph where y= priority 1 and x= priority 2, and plot job roles within the space. If you're not much of a graph sketcher, simply rank each job out of a maximum of 10 based on your chosen priorities. Which job scores highest? Does this help you compare them in a more objective way?

tl;dr

- Doing part time jobs and internships during university are a sure fire way to help you understand what you want out of your career.

- Gain as many experiences as you can to gather data about yourself in the workplace, what you're interested in, what you like and dislike, what type of people you enjoy working with. Use this information to make decisions about what jobs could be fulfilling for you.

- Be open to trying new things and doing internships at companies you've never heard of but sound interesting to you, it's through doing rather than

30

Dream Big. Hustle Hard.
reading we can find out the most about ourselves.

Chapter 4
Fear of failure and perfectionism are not your friends

- It's important for you to think critically about your motivations in life and what's really important to you career-wise.

- Assess job opportunities according to your priorities and your life goals, not your parents' / friends' / society's.

- Based on your personal motivations, create a profile of your dream job's characteristics and match the profile you've built to the jobs that are out there.

I graduated from the London School of Economics in 2009 with a BSc (Honours) in Economics and Government. My final mark was a 69. Just one mark off a First. But graduating in the height of the financial crisis meant that missing my First class degree would be just the first in a long line of disappointments. Like many young women in our patriarchal societies, I'd been raised to be a perfectionist, so anything short of perfect would always leave me feeling like I'd failed. I know what you're thinking, what does perfect mean anyway? For the younger me, it boiled down to how I was raised, in a way where perfect meant meeting my parents' very high expectations. This quest for perfectionism really instilled a fear of failure in me, which is something I've discussed with many of my close girlfriends, and women in Hustle Crew, who all agree and feel the same. The fear of failure holds us back from trying so many different things. And it takes time to shift from this limiting mindset. I would know as I spent most of my twenties trying to.

I'm a classic international school kid. I was born to parents from different parts of the world, in a country neither of them was from or raised in. I moved around a lot as a child living in different countries - The Philippines, USA, Tanzania, Kenya and Nigeria - and ended up in a boarding school in the UK in my teens. But beneath the exciting story of a jet set childhood and adolescence is a standard human being with all the same insecurities and anxieties as the next person, trying to get through this game we call life.

Born in Washington DC, I was my parent's third child, but they soon divorced. In my early years I spent the week at my mom's, a classic Filipino home where discipline was firm, white rice formed the base of most meals and attending mass on a Sunday was a given. On Friday nights we would often spend time with our dad, where we could rent anything we wanted from Blockbusters (aka Netflix for 90s kids) and have a Popeye's bucket for dinner. As an elementary school kid in American suburbia this was a dream Friday night. Disney movies and fast food - what more could a girl ask for? My dad remarried my step mum, also Nigerian, and was soon promoted to be the International Monetary Fund's Country Director in Tanzania. With the promotion came the opportunity for us to live with him full time in Africa. As an 8-year old in a suburb of DC nothing this exciting had happened since the Power Rangers first aired on TV.

Moving in with my dad was a change of order. I'd gone from being raised by my mother and live-in nanny into a patriarchal Nigerian household where education was valued very highly, if not obsessively. I often felt that in my father's eyes I was only as good as my grades, and lived in fear of

33

the repercussions of not succeeding at school. My father was born in a small town in south-western Nigeria, one of many children to a man with more than one wife. The prospects for a boy like him would be to complete his education (Nigeria was still a British colony then) and become a doctor, a lawyer, or pursue a career in the civil service or as an academic. My dad enjoyed learning and was a top pupil. He realised that getting the top grades opened doors for him. Through scholarships he was able to travel across Nigeria as a teenager and even all expenses paid to Germany. This was the late 1950s, long before you could do a quick Google search of 'weather in Berlin' and so my dad, too proud (or forgetful) to inquire about what to pack, arrived in the height of a bitter winter in traditional Nigerian attire including sandals on his feet.

My dad eventually gained a place at Balliol College, Oxford studying PPE (Politics, Philosophy and Economics) following in the footsteps of some of the greatest politicians and economists in history. He completed his doctorate at Oxford and (according to his account) only ever had one job interview, which occurred in his tutor's office with a manager from the IMF who made an offer at the end of their chat. Things have changed quite a bit since then! But all through my childhood, whenever my dad would check my report card, or ask about how I did on my latest test or assignment, he would remind me of his experiences at school, and what great things he now had as a result of his hard work.

My dad's favourite saying, which he recited to me almost weekly was, "To whom much is given, much is expected." Certainly all my material needs and more were provided for as a child. I had a great education, tutors for subjects where I wasn't getting the top grades, lavish birthday parties, all the new clothes, toys and gadgets I wanted - but the pressure to be the best was ever present. And coupled with this pressure came an intense fear of failure. Because I felt the pressure to get top grades, I became oriented around only doing things that helped that goal. Studying, reading, tutoring. I wasn't encouraged to think independently so much as I was encouraged to memorise the various syllabi of my subjects.

I remember once when I was 11 or 12 and living in Nairobi, I scored 98% on our end of year maths exam. I had missed just one mark. Our teacher created quite a suspenseful build-up to the big reveal of the results. "Someone in this classroom only missed one mark on the final paper!" We all glanced at each other wondering who it could be. "Congratulations, Aba!" he said as my classmates burst into applause. I was happy, but not as excited as my classmates were for me. Giorgio, my classmate sitting next to me, said "Wow, well done, Aba! What will your parents get you for doing that?" I replied, "Oh I don't know, probably nothing." "Nothing? Really? Wow! If I took that home I could have anything I want!" And sure enough when I did take my test paper home, proudly displaying my mark, my step-mum was very happy for me but my dad's response was to ask why I hadn't got 100%.

Having a sense of perfectionism drilled into you from a young age isn't practical. And if you're a perfectionist and it is holding you back from taking risks in your career, you might want to reassess your decision making processes. Speaking from my own experience, the obsession with getting top grades was coupled with an internal fear of failure. As I grew up it meant that I only put myself forward for things I believed I could do perfectly. 100% or nothing. Failure was not an option. But where's the value in being so black and white about what success or perfection is in a world filled with grey?

We know that high risks bring high rewards when they go right. And big losses when they go wrong. But is it worth it?

That's all up to you. I now look at life in terms of the opportunities available. I consider what I'm looking for out of a job - what will drive me, what will motivate me. I don't worry too much about whether I will be perfect. I worry more about whether or not I can work hard in the role, and do my best, learn as I'm doing and improve myself. I've learned to be happy with my best efforts, regardless of whether or not those best efforts are 'perfect' or 'top of the class'. I use one of Sheryl Sandberg's quotes as a mantra to remind myself that a perfectionist mindset is self-serving, and not in a good way. "Done is better than perfect". Reminding myself of this enables me to get more stuff done.

Remembering that done is better than perfect also enables me to share my work with others as I'm doing it, instead of being protective of it. This is an important lesson for perfectionists to learn. Through acknowledgement of my perfectionist mindset and its shortcomings I've learned that getting feedback throughout a process of working is less damaging to my ego. In the past, I would be protective of my work until I felt it was 'perfect' and ready to show the world. But that also meant I was very sensitive to any criticism of the 'perfect' work. Now I understand the value of getting feedback as I'm working, to save me time and also make me more willing to listen to feedback, while the work is still at a stage where I can easily incorporate changes.

The start of my twenties was the start of me being more autonomous and independent. It was a challenging time. When I tried to think hard about what I wanted - as the careers counsellors on campus advised me to do - the only voices I could hear were my parents. Where was my voice? Where was my desire? It was only when I became comfortable with the idea of taking risks, of pursuing an opportunity where success was not guaranteed but could be a bonus, that I felt I was really finding myself.

Activity:

- Grab a blank sheet of paper and write 'perfect' at the top.

- Now start listing the words that define what perfect means to you.

- Does the list seem reasonable? Does it seem realistic? Is it contradictory? What does 'perfect' mean anyway?

- As you grow up you create your own version of perfect based on your experiences of life, what you see and are told and your upbringing. That means perfection is actually a subjective standard completely unique to each individual. Sounds to me like perfection is pretty unattainable, and pretty undesirable.

- The values that your parents expound influence your own, whether you choose to accept them or rebel against them. So if you feel like you are a perfectionist - question that mindset and ask yourself why. What benefit does that mindset bring you? If you're anything like me than you might find, like I did, that the perfectionist mindset is more limiting than helpful.

Framework: Next time you find yourself avoiding a task, procrastinating on an important project, or not pursuing a new opportunity/challenge -- interrogate yourself for the reasons why. Could it be that you are avoiding it because you only want to do things you can be perfect at? Trying, even at risk of failing, is how you gain the experience and the learnings. Those things do not come through success.

Ask yourself - am I limiting myself through this behaviour? Dedicate time each week to improving your self-awareness and unpicking any limiting mindsets you may have developed over your lifetime so far. There are so many ways to improve self-awareness, experiment with them until you find what works for you. I enjoy meditating, writing poetry and writing my reflections. Many people I know journal regularly and say it helps them improve their self-awareness.

tl;dr

- Perfectionism is a limiting mindset which stops you from trying something new or taking risks.

- If you are a perfectionist, spend some time asking yourself why you are and what usefulness that attitude has brought you, also examine the downsides the attitude also brings   .

- It's important to create your own standards by which to judge yourself and by which to judge your success and understand what you personally find motivating and fulfilling when it comes to work.

- Get feedback on your behaviour from people whose opinion you respect e.g. professors, relatives working in the field you aspire to be in, etc. Don't be afraid to ask questions at risk of looking ignorant/stupid/pesky/annoying. Their feedback could help you find areas of development that you can't see in yourself e.g. "You care too much what others think of you!"

- Try different activities to help you improve your self-awareness on your own e.g. keeping a journal or   mindfulness.

Chapter 5
How to use the internet to help you decide your next best move

- You're fortunate to live in an age where you can easily access information to inform your career choice, so make sure you do your research.

- Exploit online resources like Glassdoor, LinkedIn and AngelList to build a holistic overview of the career options open to you.

- In tech, like many industries, the best opportunities come through networking so leverage social media and online communities to make relevant connections to get to where you want to be.

At university you will be bombarded with promotional material from various corporations who want to woo you and get you to apply to work for them. It's great to get the free pens but make sure you do your research. There are millions of companies around the world that you could work for. There are tens of thousands of types of jobs across dozens of industries that you can do. Possibilities are almost endless. So explore as many of the possibilities as you can before you decide. Don't apply to a company you don't know much about on a whim - you may find out that you really don't like their mission, their culture or their staff.

You can use resources like Glassdoor, LinkedIn, and more informal blogs and Twitter accounts to build a layered profile of a company and what it's like to work there. Google News is a great way to see what the press is saying, both good and bad. Type in the company name and look to see what the latest articles are saying. Look for indicators that the company is doing well. Happy results mean they are working effectively as a team, and it also means it could be a positive environment to work in. It could also mean they have a very effective PR machine so be comprehensive in your research, using multiple sources. On a more material level, happy results also mean that the company is financially healthy and that you would likely have good job security if you landed a role there.

In the startup world particularly, many companies fail. While that is part and parcel of the sector and certainly not a bad thing on your CV, it could be a bad thing for your bank balance and is a risk you must accept when taking on a startup role. But doing research helps you understand the risks and mitigate better. Crunchbase is a pretty comprehensive investor database that lets you search for companies and find out information including how much funding they've received, who their investors are and who is in their founding team. It's not 100 percent accurate but helps you paint a picture.

Also check out what TechCrunch and other reputable blogs like The Verge, Wired and Forbes have to say. Are there any conferences or lectures the founder has spoken at that you can watch on YouTube? I personally find that I absorb information most effectively through video, and love searching for information on companies through YouTube or Google Video. I'll usually be able to find someone from their leadership team speaking in an interview or on a panel. I'll occasionally find in-house videos that they have created, which are a good way to get a better insight into their values and branding. It also creates a useful talking point.

LinkedIn is also great for spotting what kind of people are already in the organisation. You can see who is in what role

- you can scope out the diversity of the team, as well as their backgrounds and career paths. Looking at their career paths can give you pointers about how you can best position yourself to join the company if you're interested. For example, is there any commonality between you and the staff already there? Similar degrees? Universities? Languages? Internships? Doing this investigation will be helpful because if you do find some connection or overlap, that creates an opportunity for you to spark a conversation. For example, if you share a network - you could leverage your connections to get a personal introduction. Use the introduction to get their advice about your career planning. As I say again in a future chapter - ask questions that Google can't answer. Questions like, 'what is a typical day for you like?', 'how has the company changed since you joined?' and 'what do you enjoy most about working there?'.

Be sure to ask the questions that fill in the blanks of the picture you're painting in your head. You want to be as certain as you can that this opportunity is right for you, so think of exactly what you want to know about the job and company that will help you decide. Ultimately, what is most important about the job, comes down to you. What makes you tick, what makes you excited and what makes you feel motivated?

Don't get too hung up on whether it fits into your long-term plan, or whether it narrows down future options. As I'll elaborate on in the next chapters - personal branding is what enables us to turn any collection of experiences into a powerful story that can secure us any job. It's all about selling your transferable skills as applied to future roles. It's not so much about what you did. What's more important is how you did it. As Steve Jobs said, 'you can only connect the dots looking backwards.'

Let's put ourselves in the hiring manager's shoes for a

41

moment, to understand why these tips are so useful and effective for jobseekers. A hiring manager writes a job description knowing what kind of person she wants to work with. She knows what has to be done in this role, how this role helps her and makes her day at work a little easier. When she writes the description she doesn't have a clear image in her mind of who that ideal candidate will be. In fact, she feels like it could be lots of different people. People study for different degrees, have different strengths and life experiences. As long as these combine to create someone suited to the requirements, she's open to the idea of them joining her team.

Given there's no cookie-cutter carbon copy candidate - you as the applicant have the opportunity to shape your CV to match their job requirements. Present yourself as the candidate they are looking for. It's your responsibility to frame your experiences in the context of their requirements - so that the transferable skills and strengths you have acquired throughout your life so far, clearly stand out and show your abilities to do the role. If you think this sounds far-fetched - it's not.

When I worked at Groupon we had the most effective Partner Management team across the whole company, which was operating in over 40 countries at the time. Quarter after quarter we beat our merchant satisfaction targets. If you look at what the requirements are of a good Partner Manager - you might think that this amazing performance came from a consistent stock of similar graduates. In reality, we were a rag-tag bunch from different backgrounds, with different academic credentials. Although a fair few came from the usual haunts like LSE, most others came from universities across the UK and further afield, having studied a variety of subjects at university and some had even graduated with 2.2s.

If you still have questions about what to do, then you need to collect more data. Go online, and find out more that you haven't already answered. Make a document listing companies that interest you relating to their mission, values, product or services. Can you read about people who work there? Are any of them on social media - blogging on Medium or ranting on Twitter? What can you find out about the working environment through them? Is there anyone you can speak to in a similar role or in a similar organisation? Remember that most people are willing to give you advice about their job or company if you ask them kindly and earnestly. Massage their ego and it will make them even more approachable and likely to respond. People tend to enjoy helping others giving advice. Don't feel shy. The worst thing that could happen is that they don't reply. And don't tell me that you've never failed to reply to an email?

Consider using Twitter to approach someone initially, perhaps in response to a tweet they made. Or tweet them to get their contact details so you may ask them more directly in private, if you're unable to find their email address anywhere online. You'll notice from exploring the platform that there is something about Twitter that makes it a great leveller. Ordinary strangers interact with world legends - you can directly access record-breaking musicians or Olympic athletes - and more importantly CEOs, founders and thought leaders.

Here are some more tactics you can try to leverage online communities and professional networks to help you land the jobs you want:

AngelList:

AngelList is a great hiring platform for the startup world. It's a platform where entrepreneurs connect with potential investors, advisors, employees and any other connections within the startup ecosystem. Like LinkedIn, it operates like a social media platform. You must complete a profile and, once done, you can add connections and apply for jobs. Make your profile concise (most people have very short attention spans and are put off by large blocks of text) and be sure to include all your key achievements, quantifying as much as possible e.g. if you're an aspiring copywriter who's been writing for the student newspaper you could add a bullet point headline saying "Published 50+ articles as News Editor for university student newspaper." You can set your status on Angel List to be specific about the types of interactions you're looking for e.g. 'Looking for a job' or 'interested in a coffee date'. Like all websites, features change regularly, so be sure to spend some time on the platform exploring all the pages and features to become familiar with them and maximise them to your advantage.

Twitter:

If you're new to Twitter set up an account and think about who you want to follow. If you know the industry or sector you are interested in working in you can get lists, through search engines, of the most influential people in that field on Twitter. Go through the list and follow them all, see what they're saying. What articles are they quoting? What do they write about? Is there an opportunity for you to engage with them in a relevant and meaningful way? In a way which relates to your career goal? If you've enjoyed one of their recent blog posts, you could retweet it with a specific recommendation e.g. 'great sales advice for #startup #femalefounders'. Use hashtags of keywords to draw other users interested in these fields to your content, it creates more opportunities to engage with like-minded people who could further your career goals. You may notice Twitter users interacting with you, by liking your tweets or re-tweeting you or even sending you a direct message to start a conversation. Twitter is a great way for people across the world with a common interest to communicate and share engaging content. I've met lots of interesting, valuable contacts through Twitter and in the early days of Hustle Crew it was a great way to grow a community relevant to our mission of promoting diversity in tech.

Local jobs boards, interest groups and communities:

In the U.K. www.workinstartups.com is a popular portal for tech startup jobs, but there are always new websites and communities cropping up advertising startup roles. Jobs boards for the tech industry are often focused on a specific type of role e.g. engineering, or a specific demographic e.g. women (www.shecancode.io) or people of colour (http://www.peopleofcolorintech.com). There are often local careers communities that you can find through Twitter, Facebook, Medium, Slack or other social networks or communication platforms. These may be communities focused on a specific skill-set or discipline e.g. Data Science or UX/ UI design. Spend some time on search engines, or search on social media platforms, to find out if there are any local jobs groups near you that post job roles out to their community. In the UK we have grassroots careers groups focused on empowering specific groups of individuals e.g. Black Girl Tech (specifically for black women interested in coding and securing engineering roles in future, although men are a part of the community too), Geek Girl Meetup (for anyone interested in tech and digital careers and promoting diversity in the space) and YSYS (for young people interested in startups and entrepreneurship).

How to organise your information:

As you do your job research you are likely to be overwhelmed with information. I know I was. I used to scribble down notes on loose sheets of paper, or into the closest notepad or notebook I could find. But then I would forget exactly where I wrote what and would get frustrated. Thankfully, now the cloud exists it's a lot easier to store information in one single place that you can access from multiple devices. I'm a huge fan of Google Docs which are free to use, but there are plenty of alternatives online. For jobs information I like to use Google Sheets, where each column has a heading for the specific type of information I am saving e.g. Company Name, Job Title, Office Location, Company Values etc.

The advantage of using Google Sheets is that, like Excel, you can apply filters to help you narrow down data based on specific criteria e.g. you may want to use a Google Sheet to list in every row all the jobs you are interested in applying for and include a column which shows whether you have sent off your application or not. Then you can filter down to show only jobs where you have not yet sent the application to have a quick glance at how much work you have ahead of you!

People often ask me about the best way to organise their job information or to track progress and I will say it really depends. It depends on your working style and what tools are easiest for you. I love spreadsheets because I'm a nerd like that, you might detest them. Maybe you'd rather keep your data in a Word doc, or in a more visual graph or table that you build in PowerPoint / Keynote. The purpose of organising it is to make it easy for you to keep tabs on your progress, and not get discouraged or overwhelmed. So find the method that suits you best. You may decide to keep it completely offline and simply have one notebook dedicated to all things job related. If so, that's fine. Just make sure you don't lose it!

Final thoughts on using the internet for job research:

Most of the information you need to make a decision is out there, it's all about investing the time to do your research. Treat the research like you would your dissertation or any other project that is really important to you. The reality is there is no such thing as a perfect plan. Even the best laid out plan will fall subject to setbacks. Why? Because that's life, you cannot control everything. You cannot mitigate every risk and you cannot control every variable. Even if you are determined to be the most successful tech entrepreneur, with a 100 billion dollar IPO, you must remember that so many parts of that happy ending are beyond your control.

Yes, you can work hard to build an incredible organisation, but success and the happy ending depend on so many other variables e.g. your customers, your employees, your investors, the economic climate. The list goes on. There are numerous stakeholders who all have different, often competing, needs and whose actions will determine whether or not your company succeeds. That's why it's really important to have your own personal definition of success, not one which is contingent on external factors. My personal definition of success in this moment in time is to make a positive impact on the lives of people I care about. I measure that through the feedback I receive from the Hustle Crew community. I'm open to revising this definition in time, if and when my priorities and perspectives change. Remember that the startup game moves quickly, so the most useful tools to help you will be changing all the time, this book is not an exhaustive reference, but comprehensive enough for you get the ball rolling.

Activity:
- How can you find out what a typical day in a prospective company is like? Let's call it Company A. It will be difficult to get honest, warts and all accounts from Company A's corporate careers pages or recruiters. Is there anyone in your school or personal network who used to work for Company   A?

- Once you have a shortlist of dream employers lined up, leverage your university and personal network, asking if anyone knows anyone who used to work there and would be willing to chat to you, off the record, about their experiences. Be clear that it's simply to help you decide if it's a good fit.

- Before you start chatting with them, think about what is important to you in the employer-employee relationship, and use that as the basis of the conversation. If you are interested in opportunities to learn on the job you could ask what training support they received while they worked there. This will be particularly important if you're joining entry-level, so be sure to ask questions about what the work experience is like for entry-level employees.

Framework:

Return to your notes on your career priorities. What matters most to you when it comes to jobs. Is it compensation? Is it the distance between the office and your home? Is it the international reach of the employer? List all the deciding factors in a holistic way, covering every aspect of work: dress code, commute, co-workers, office layout etc. and as you research roles be sure to make note of how each opportunity rates along your preferences. You may choose to have 5 deciding factors and rate each company you are considering out of 10 on each factor. Tally your scores to see which companies come out on top. Doing this helps you make data-driven, more objective decisions about job choices. Gather consistent data so you can compare jobs and companies as objectively as possible. This is why I find using a spreadsheet to store information very useful.

tl;dr

- Conduct your job hunt research with the same level of critical analysis and thoroughness as your thesis or any other key research project.

- Leverage all the relevant resources that are out there to get a rounded opinion - from jobs boards to social media channels to budding careers communities.

- Organise yourself so that the information you gather is easy to comprehend and review, use tools that let you save on the cloud if you find that helpful, or stick with a medium that works best for you.

PART II: CRAFTING YOUR NARRATIVE, PERSONAL BRANDING AND CULTIVATING CONFIDENCE

Chapter 6
Showing off your accomplishments is an awkward necessity in the job market

- Cultivate a list of your best skills, strengths and assets and get comfortable showing off about them.

- Your CV is a list of accomplishments you've earned, so be proud to show them off.

- You have to be your number one fan, if not, who else will be?

- How can you convince your employer you're the perfect candidate if you don't believe you are?

Studies have shown that as women we downplay our success and accomplishments far more than men. A woman founder I greatly admire even recently said in an interview that "women are too honest." In a job hunting scenario, this behaviour can be extremely detrimental to our desired outcomes. One of my most memorable lectures at LSE happened in a behavioural economics course. Our professor was educating us on asymmetries of information and the theory of signalling. To illustrate the theory's principles he used the examples of toads during mating season. Male toads croak to attract a mate, the idea being that the bigger and deeper your croak, the bigger your body, suggesting you are a robust mate, attractive to females. It was an example to illustrate the importance of how you communicate about yourself to the world, including those who are yet to see

51

you. I use this analogy a lot in the careers workshops I run with students to remind them that, even though it may feel awkward, showing off about your achievements is an important part of interviews and recruitment events.

I always found it helpful to remind myself that the job market was precisely that - a market. All the candidates like me provided the supply side, and all the tech companies with vacancies formed the demand side. If I'm going after the same role as all the dozens of other possible candidates out there then it's really important that I give myself the best possible chance for success as I compete for the one open spot. How can I do that? By ensuring I'm knowledgeable about the role and its requirements and by explicitly portraying how my experiences to date and skills match the employers' needs perfectly. It's like a matching system, except in this case, we are not operating in a world with perfect information, meaning we have to do a lot more work to make this go our way. This is where you need to turn up your hustle. There are so many elements to your personality and life experiences that make you unique. Turn those elements into assets and be proud of how these experiences have shaped you and how you view the world. Perhaps they have given you a unique perspective for approaching problems, building relationships or anything else the world of work may throw your way!

One of my favourite sayings when it comes to job-hunting is 'failing to prepare is preparing to fail' and in the tricky world of job hunting and interviewing that really rings true. You might know and believe in your heart that you are the perfect candidate for the position, but if you don't take the time and consideration diligently to research the position and the organisation, how can you know for sure? And even if you do all of that, and you have a clear idea that you'd excel in the role, if you don't make it explicit and sell all your relevant skills without holding back, how will the hiring managers know? There's another reason why it's so important to do as much research and preparation as you can before an interview. I know from myself and my friends that ambitious/perfectionist/women are extremely hard on themselves. I am often my worst critic and even though I'm aware of this challenge, it doesn't make my inner voice any less critical, harsh or judgemental. What I've learned is that doing everything I absolutely can to prepare for something makes coping with failure easier. If I truly feel I tried my best, and things still don't go my way, I can put the blame on any of the numerous other variables that affected the outcome.

Fear. What exactly are we afraid of? Has living in a patriarchy where we are constantly objectified and vilified and paid less than our male peers for doing the same job (if not a better one) made us afraid really to be ourselves? To tap into our heart's desires and try to turn them into reality? Perhaps. But surely just by starting to be mindful of these limitations, and doing everything in our power to fight them, we can start to turn that fear from a crippling emotion into a catalyst. A year ago I quit my job with no next move planned. I was the most scared I had ever been in my entire life. I feared the judgement I would receive from family, friends, and even people I didn't really know but whose opinions matter for some irrational reason. When I decided to launch Hustle Crew it was the beginning of a journey where I consciously conquered my fears. Now I do things I'm afraid of on an almost daily basis. The nervousness never goes away, you just get more used to it. I am certain that by doing things I'm afraid of I have become more resilient. And if I can do it, so can you.

Activity:
- Each person has an individual strength, skill or attribute that distinguishes them from others. Tapping into your special skills will help you build

your confidence.

- If you're not sure what those special skills are, start by asking what you are good at from the people closest to you. Pick five people you have a good relationship with - they could be friends, family, teachers, sports coaches.

- You could write each person a note, by email or text message, telling them that you're working through this careers skills book and one activity asked that you ask them for their opinion on what your best skills are.

- The responses may not correlate to a career path in an obvious way, but it will help boost your self-belief. Analyse the responses you get, and see what insights you can draw from them about the transferable skills you possess.

- Your best friends may tell you that you are their favourite person to go to for advice because you're a great listener and problem solver. These are both valuable skills showing your ability to communicate and analyse information, skills which can be used in a variety of roles.

- Grab a blank sheet of paper and sketch a mind map. Put your name in the middle and draw lines out from it that end with words from the responses you receive. You now have a visualisation of all your natural abilities and strengths.

- Think of how each could be useful in the range of job opportunities that appeal to you.

Framework:

If you still find it difficult to get yourself into the mindset of showing off about your achievements, take a step back and put yourself in the shoes of a hiring manager or recruiter. Remember that the job market is flooded with talented candidates. As a hiring manager, how can I decide which person is best for the role? I have only the information which applicants give me. So if two applicants have identical grades from identical schools, how will I distinguish between them? It might be that one candidate does a better job of clarifying how they have excelled, and how they are distinguishable from their peers. This candidate, who has done a better job of selling them self, suddenly stands out to me, and I want to call them in for an interview. Always put yourself in the mindset of the hiring manager or recruiter when you are presenting information to help your chances of landing the job.

tl;dr

- Don't be reluctant to share your accomplishments. You worked hard for them and they are critical data points that will help you beat the competition in the recruitment process.

- Hiring managers aren't mind readers. Unless you are explicit about what you have achieved and what you can achieve, you may lose out to the competition who are better at selling themselves.

- There is no perfect next step or bad decision you can make at the beginning of your career. Focus on your high-level goal and appreciate that many paths and opportunities can lead you there.

Chapter 7
What's your elevator pitch? Your headline story? Networking like a pro

- A compelling answer to 'tell me a little about yourself' helps open doors, so ensure you practice one you can easily roll off the tongue in networking situations.

- Use your intro to set the scene for why you're the right person for their team whenever you meet a relevant contact at a job fair or event.

- Start to understand the simple dynamics of sales and how you can leverage them in networking situations to your advantage.

- "Good things happen to those who hustle." - Anais Nin.

If you've watched The Apprentice, Dragon's Den or any sort of entrepreneur focused show, you're probably familiar with the elevator pitch. It's essentially a pitch you give to a key stakeholder like a future boss or investor, that would convince them to say yes in the time it takes from boarding the elevator in the lobby to reaching the floor of their office. It's an exercise that forces you to focus on your unique and most compelling selling points, as well as making you address the specific pertinent facts relating to your business in as concise a way as possible It also requires incredible story-telling abilities. In the competitive job market, all graduates face today it's important that you have your individual elevator pitch. Why is this important? At any point in time you may come across a gatekeeper - at a recruitment fair or even on a phone screen call. You will almost certainly be asked to tell them a little bit about yourself. If you're really serious about standing out you will want to prepare a rehearsed answer to this question so that you can reel off with ease the most compelling selling points about yourself and your experience.

When I was still at university I hadn't developed the obsession with reading careers books and articles I have today. I really was just bumbling along doing my best to keep my head above water in the classroom and keep my head out of the loo after heavy nights at the students' union. As such, I approached careers events with little or no preparation. It should come as no surprise that those events never really amounted to anything. Because I hadn't done my research, I never knew what questions to ask and I never knew which contact details to take. As I got older I realised how valuable these opportunities were. Most big organisations have automated systems set up to filter out job applications, and yet at a careers event you can come face to face with someone from the recruitment team or, even better, someone working in the team you'd like to join. I only began to connect the dots later and realise how getting the right contact face to face could increase the chances of my application being successful.

It's not enough just to show up at these events and come face to face with a company representative. You must be prepared to introduce yourself in a clear and concise way so you make a great first impression. This is important for phone screen interviews, too. It wouldn't be a great idea to spend your intro rambling on about what star sign you were born under and what you had for breakfast. That is not the information hiring managers are looking for when they say, 'tell me a little about yourself'. They want you to tell them a little bit about yourself in the context of the situation i.e. the job you are applying for. This is why preparation is so important. Your introduction is a mini sales pitch and if you get it right you can make a strong first impression that will set you apart from the crowd. Start by thinking about what skills and experiences you have that are most relevant for the opportunity. E.g. if it's a digital marketing conference you may want to boast your 10k-strong community of followers on Instagram and Twitter, and that you're obsessed with connecting with people across social media and using entertaining content to build bridges across the world wide web and making thoughtful connections with people.

If you dissect your elevator pitch it should not only say something about you, it should ideally have something quantifiable which puts your points into context. Consider the difference between saying "I'm interested in digital marketing because I love social media and I have lots of Twitter followers" and "I'm interested in digital marketing because I love social media and even have 15,000 Twitter followers on an account I started ten months ago". Immediately, the statement with a quantitative point has more credibility and context. Remember that the people you are speaking to - recruiters, employees, hiring managers - are speaking to hundreds of prospective candidates all the time. You can imagine how all the conversations might start to blend into one long stream of information. To set yourself apart, you need to deliver compelling concrete facts in your statement, almost as a data point they can anchor on to. Saying "I did well in my media studies A-level" isn't as powerful or memorable as saying "I scored the highest in my school and county in my media studies A-level".

It's important that your enthusiasm for the role/field comes across in your intro. I've never really liked using the word 'passionate' but still struggle to find anything better to replace it. You can use 'obsessed' in the right context. For example I've seen startups advertise for people 'obsessed with customer service/product/growth hacking' etc. But make sure you know your audience. If you're speaking to someone from a more formal industry, using the word obsessed may suggest a mental imbalance that they are not comfortable dealing with. If you know specifics about their company e.g. a new product they've released or an interesting TED talk their founder made, you could use this in your intro. You might want to wrap up your elevator pitch saying something like, "I've been inspired to work for you since reading [insert CEO's name] book on x,y,z, because it's such a daring and unique approach to marketing that I think other brands would be too scared to try".

At the end of your intro you want the person on the other end of the conversation to feel like they would be silly not to carry on this conversation further. You want them to feel as though, if they don't give you a chance and their competitor does, they may be paying the price later. In sales there is a common theory that people act based on two emotions - fear and greed. If that's true, you want your elevator pitch to make people fear the consequences of their competitor hiring you, or appeal to their greed, making them feel like hiring you would be gaining an asset that helps their company grow quicker. It takes a long time to develop a line that rolls off the tongue, so don't put pressure on yourself to find a perfect one right off the bat. I like listening to what other people say when they introduce themselves in networking events or speaking events, and even copy lines I like. Feel free to do the same, imitation is the sincerest form of flattery after all.

Activity:
- Grab a sheet of paper and list in bullet points, all the compelling facts about yourself as a job candidate.

- For each role/company you are interested in working for, grab the three most compelling facts from the list and arrange them into a powerful one-liner.

- Practice the different one-liners until you have one you would be confident using at a networking event.

Framework:

- Know your audience and engage in a tone suitable to the situation and environment.

- Practice your intros in advance so you have confidence when meeting new contacts.

- Leave lasting positive impressions with those you meet. Take their contact details in case you can name them in a future job application.

- Be conscious of your listening/speaking ratio: ensure you're using the opportunity to ask questions and listen to their responses. View the interaction more as a fact-finding mission than a sales pitch, ideally 70% listening to 30% talking.

tl;dr

- Having a compelling intro ready prepared in your mind makes networking and cold meet ups that little bit less awkward. So, practice a few in the comfort of your own home.

- First impressions have a huge impact, so practicing your one-liner maximises your opportunity to create a positive, impactful first impression.

- Be sure to keep your audience in mind when you introduce yourself and use language appropriate for the person and situation, particularly when considering the formality of your tone.

- Keep it short and sweet and remember that listening is a very important part of networking, especially at the start of your career. Maintain a good listening ratio (e.g. speak only 20-30% of the conversation) and ask lots of questions.

Chapter 8
Coffee date etiquette and how to find a mentor

- Coffee dates are a great way to find out more about an industry from the people in it and get relevant advice on the best way to get hired, possibly even get   referred.

- Take the lead on arranging times to meet so it's as easy as possible for people to say yes to your offer.

- Never ask someone to be your mentor outright, instead cultivate a valuable relationship like you're friends.

- Make the most of 1-on-1s by doing as much research as you can yourself and saving questions which need expert / specialist advice.

In this chapter we'll cover the best way to secure, prepare for and behave in key interactions including coffee dates, meet-ups and mentor meetings. Coffee dates are an effective way to meet new connections and find out more about a potential industry, company or role you're interested in. They tend to be informal and follow a cold introduction made by a friend or acquaintance. I found myself one summer thinking of making a move into venture capital. A relatively new industry which started about 50 years ago it remains small and a famously tough nut to crack. Most VC jobs are gained through networking as it's a tight-knit community hardly known for its inclusivity. I knew a few venture firms in London and remembered that one of my good friends had come close to getting a VC job a few years back, and figured he could be of help. He kindly offered to make some introductions over email which I could follow up to schedule coffee dates. But before any of those coffee dates, I did my research online, read a few books, made lots of notes and then decided I was ready to meet people in the industry. There were things I was curious about that my research could not help answer, so the coffee dates presented an opportunity for me to gain a better understanding of what the day-to-day of being in VC looked like. One of the coffee dates I met was so impressed by my research and experience that at the end of our date he offered to show my CV to one of the partners regarding a vacancy they had.

When asking for help it's really important that you make it as easy as possible for the person you are asking to help you. You don't want to annoy or frustrate them by asking something trivial or making even the slightest suggestion you are unprepared and don't value their time. For example, if you're interested in finding out more about an industry, exhaust all the resources at your disposal first, so that when you go to seek help, you've already got the basics covered. Time is a precious commodity, so if someone kindly offers you their time, you want to show them that you value it. You do that by being prepared well in advance, and asking questions which show you have prepared and done your own initial research prior to the meeting.

This is important because if you arrive prepared for that initial contact it shows just how serious and committed you are to the goal. It makes an incredible first impression on this person who could open doors for you in your career. It also means that whatever questions you have left to ask must be those really crucial, personal ones that you couldn't find online or in books. Questions which are really important to you like "what's a typical day like at X firm?"

"What's it like to work for X partner?" These are questions which are often the most interesting to answer.

By doing your research before approaching a friend or acquaintance for more insight or intros, you're demonstrating that you're really serious and committed because you've done the research before. It's also a sign of respect. Time is a precious commodity, something of which we have a finite amount but always want more of. Think about it - imagine a friend at university asked you to help them with their essay. You arrange a time to meet, you sit in the cafe, and they open up their laptop. In front of them is a blank page. You ask - where's the essay you want me to look at? They answer - I haven't started it. You might be a bit annoyed. It's the exact same thing if you suddenly decide you want to become a film producer, tell a friend, and they introduce you to a contact of theirs who's in the film industry. If you show up at that meeting and ask 'so what do film producers do?' they might be within their rights to walk straight out of the cafe and end the meeting right there. You could type that same question into Google and get millions of answers.

Older people I come across who are in senior or executive roles at large corporates often ask me why so many young people seem to have a sense of entitlement when it comes to careers help. Just the other day I was talking about the mentoring work I do at Hustle Crew to a middle aged senior executive at a world-renowned consulting firm when I was asked, "Oh but don't so many young people have an expectation that they're owed unlimited time, help, etc. to enable them achieve their ambitions?" I didn't quite know what to say. It is probably the classic case of older generations lambasting the younger ones but, either way, it's a mindset that exists, so do everything in your power not to perpetuate it. Challenge those negative expectations by being extremely well prepared and well researched. In the age of the internet there is really no excuse.

From an administrative perspective, logistics around coffee dates and meetups can often be tedious and annoying. You certainly want to take the lead in arranging the day and time to meet and clarifying what you would like to discuss in the meetup. If you are reaching out asking for help from someone you know directly, start by calling them on their mobile to have a simple conversation where you can settle this. If you don't know them well enough to call them, or fear they may be busy, write a concise email explaining what you need help with. Include the exact dates and times over the next two weeks when you are available to chat and even suggest convenient locations. You could follow up with a text or WhatsApp to let them know you have emailed them (since most people's inboxes are flooded with new emails every day).

If you are arranging a coffee date with a friend of a friend, or someone you have been introduced to over email, respond as quickly as you can, thanking the person for taking the time to meet with you and then make a suggestion to meet for a 30 minute coffee near their office. Aim for a 30 minute meeting, at the very maximum one hour. But 30 minutes is more respectful and should be enough to cover your most burning questions. To avoid playing email tennis and bouncing around different dates use a free scheduling tool like Calendly or Mixmax. This makes it a lot easier to pin down a time that works for both parties. Include your Calendly link in your email. Here is a suggested draft you could start with:

"Thank you so much for agreeing to meet with me and share advice on how to break into X industry. I've done lots of online research but still have some questions. I'd be happy to come to your offices for a 30 minute chat in the next couple of weeks. Here is a link to my availability [insert link], please pick the time that suits you best and I will send a calendar invite. I look forward to meeting you."

Alternatively, if you are not using a calendar tool, you must write back with dates and times when you are available to meet e.g.

"Thank you so much for agreeing to meet with me and share advice on how to break into X industry. I've done lots of online research but still have some questions. I'd be happy to come to your offices for a 30 minute chat in the next couple of weeks.

I am available: Wed 5th, Thu 6th, Fri 7th, 3pm - 7pm
Please let me know which slot suits you best and I will send a calendar invite. I look forward to meeting you."

Like an interview, be sure to arrive at the coffee date with time to spare and bring your notebook so you can take notes. Think about what you want to ask before you get there. Take ownership of the meeting since you are the one who requested it. You might want to start by thanking them for their time and then stating what you want to get from the meeting e.g. "There are three things which I am really stuck on and I would love to hear your advice about them. The three things are..." Remain professional even though this is an informal meeting. You want the person to leave with a positive impression of you. You also don't want to embarrass the friend or relative who kindly made the introduction in the first place. Be yourself - the best version of yourself. Be kind, be friendly and emanate positive energy. If the person seems busy or distracted, don't take it personally, just stay focused on what you want to get out of the meeting.

You don't always have to meet face-to-face, although that is preferable. If the person you are seeking advice from is really busy e.g. hasn't responded to your emails about meeting, you could write back suggesting that you connect on a call instead. Again, send your calendar link or suggest specific dates and times you are free and include your mobile number. As they are busy it would also be wise to reiterate in your message exactly what you want to cover in the call. I have often been put off taking a call with someone when it is clear to me they are not sure what they want to talk about or how I can help them. It's a waste of my time to try and help someone who doesn't know what they need help with. Perhaps by giving greater clarity about what you need help with and why they are the best person to provide it, you warm them up to the idea and get their commitment.

It could be the case that your first coffee date/call request goes unanswered. Don't take it personally, people always have a number of priorities they are juggling at one time and you are almost certainly not one of them. Do you answer every email you receive? These things happen. It is not impolite to chase people so if you have not received a response, send a follow-up email. I usually chase three separate times before I give up. Then I return to the email conversation a month or so later if I still want to meet.

Following your coffee date or call, be sure to send a quick follow-up note, thanking them for their time. If they offered to help you in the future, return to that email thread when you need their assistance. If anything came up in your conversation that you wanted to share e.g. an interesting article - be sure to do so in the follow-up email. If the connection you have now made seems like one that will be valuable to you, continue to send them interesting articles relating to the topics you discussed so you can slowly build the relationship over time and potentially make them a mentor.

How to find a mentor and manage the relationship:

I am often asked how to find a mentor. From my experience, and from being asked to mentor many times, I think I've got the best tactic. First of all find someone whom you admire, someone you can learn from. They may be a senior person who is further along on the career journey you want, or it may be a peer who possesses incredible skills that you want to develop and grow in yourself. You can have as many mentors as you need or want, I have dozens. Some of them are friends and some of them are people I've met at networking events or who I have built a relationship with through social media and online interactions.

Once you have your list of ideal mentors, you have to think about how you can kick off the relationship. My advice is to think of this as the beginning of a friendship not the beginning of a mentorship. When you first started university how did you make friends? Did you walk up to the people you found interesting and plainly ask them? Unlikely. At least I didn't. So why would you email/tweet/approach someone and right off ask them to be your mentor? You're more likely to create a value-adding relationship if you start off slowly and simply try to have a meaningful interaction with them. Let's say there is a senior person in your office you would love as a mentor. Firstly, do your research. Find out as much as you can about them. Use this research as the starting point for your first conversation. What can you ask them, about work or their experiences that only they could answer? Avoid asking generic questions that you can get answers to online. Ask them questions which speak to their passions or projects.

Think about ways that you can help them so the relationship is mutually beneficial from the start. If it's someone at work perhaps they are working on a project you can assist with. Or if there is an opening on their team, you could volunteer to share the post across your networks or even suggest a specific friend or acquaintance who could be a relevant fit. You want to give the impression that you are a thoughtful and considerate person. In turn, the person you are helping will be thoughtful and considerate to you. They will give you the advice you need or be a sounding board for thoughts you might have. Build the relationship slowly over time with these frequent value-adding exchanges. At some point, it will make sense for you to schedule time together to catch up on things over lunch or coffee. During your catch up, be sure to be honest about the challenges you are facing that you feel they could help with.

People love being asked for advice, especially when it falls on grateful ears. Engage with the guidance you are being given and thank this person for their time. At the end of your coffee date, ask if you could catch up again in a month's time. Take ownership of setting the date and time, and sending out the calendar invite so it's a plan that actually happens instead of fading into the ether. Commit to regular meetings, and always remember that it is a two-way dynamic, where you are also giving help, advice and sharing perspectives. If you do all this, you have got yourself a mentor. Mentors are simply people who you can learn from, people who can help you overcome challenges and make progress in your career. They also help you stay accountable to your goals. Don't limit yourself to one, have a range of mentors amongst your friends, family and professional life, to inspire you and give you the momentum to keep moving forward. If you feel like there are no suitable mentors in your immediate surroundings, go to professional meet-ups or networking events to find the relevant, inspiring people and use the same approach outlined above.

Sometimes mentor relationships break down over time. Don't take it personally. We will never fully know what is happening in someone else's life, just as we can be surprised by our own feelings and decisions. Be mindful of the subtle signals that someone does not have spare time to give to you. Perhaps they haven't answered your last few emails about meeting up, or perhaps they have been reluctant to pin down a specific time or date. If you've chased the matter three times with no positive outcome, you could drop them a note saying something like:

"I can appreciate you're super busy at the moment so I will make a note to touch base with you again in a couple of months when hopefully things have calmed down a bit. Thanks for all your help so far".

Then set a reminder in your calendar or diary to notify you of two months from that email, so you can reach out again as promised. As you progress in your career your ambitions and goals will change, that's natural. That also means that the people who are ideal mentors for you may change too. Always be mindful of what your mid-term and long-term career goals are, conscious that they are flexible, as you can't control every single variable that will determine your future, and with your mind on these goals think about what value a mentor could add. You might want advice on how to navigate an industry in which you are a minority. You might want advice on how to develop a skill you see as essential but which you are not strong in. As much as possible try to gain an understanding of your strengths and weaknesses and use mentorship to help you improve on your weaknesses and learn how to harness your strengths.

At workshops I facilitated in universities I've been asked how to ask someone to be your mentor if you don't know them. I really wouldn't advise this. Not only because it's unlikely they will be willing to do it, but because valuable mentorship is context-driven. You want your mentor to know you relatively well, so they can give you relevant advice which is actionable and will make an impact. While it makes sense to look to people you admire for mentorship, apply some common sense to that perspective. You have far more to gain by asking someone you can meet in real life and get to know, than asking a complete stranger for advice. Also think about it in terms of my recommended approach for getting a mentor. I have recommended you build a friendship, an actual relationship, over time. In your eyes you have a mentor, but in their eyes you're just friends. It would be a lot harder to take this approach with someone you don't know. How would you make that initial connection and build it from there? You might be making life unnecessarily hard for yourself by trying this.

Activity:
- Make a list of your strengths and weaknesses. If you're struggling to think of them, ask nice people who you are close to and trust them to help you.

- Looking at your weaknesses, think about people you know or who you have come across who you could learn from to improve on your weaknesses.

- In your notepad, jot down a strategy for starting to build a closer relationship with them to seek their advice and mentorship. Will you offer to help them with something they are working on? Invite them to a relevant talk or industry event you are attending?

- Set a date by which you will put your plan into action so you have accountability. Note the date in your calendar or diary as a reminder.

Framework:
The best 1-on-1 interactions occur when there is mutual respect and benefit. Consider this as you approach your coffee dates and prospective mentors. Do your research, come prepared, and anticipate ways that you can contribute to the relationship and help the other person.

tl;dr
- There are best practices when it comes to coffee date etiquette. Take ownership of arranging the time and date and make it easy for the other party to confirm availability by using scheduling tools or

providing a range of possible dates and times you can do in your very first communication.

- Don't ask someone to be your mentor, instead build a friendship naturally over time with someone who you respect and admire and could learn from.

- Build a collection of mentors so you have a number of people to inspire you, to learn from, and to keep you accountable to your career goals.

- In every 1-to-1 interaction, do your best to contribute to the exchange in a positive way.

- Always follow up afterwards to give thanks and also keep the relationship moving forward.

Chapter 9
How to use your CV as a personal branding, storytelling tool

- Your CV is like a tapestry you weave. The threads are all your experiences and you choose which experiences to share based on the requirement of the role.

- Your CV should be dynamic and adaptable, a living document that you tailor to each individual role you apply for.

- Keep cover letters brief and let them show you've done your research on the company and the role.

When I first graduated the world was gripped by a recession as a result of the financial crisis. Typically an LSE economics graduate might expect to have their pick from any jobs available. This was the whole reason I slogged through the final years of secondary school to make the grade. That was the deal that you made with life: get the grades, get into the great university and bada bing bada boom, land the dollar bills in a great job. But the investment bankers of the world had other ideas and so I found myself refreshing jobs-listing page after jobs-listing page finding no inspiration, and instead looking in amazement at endless job ads for recruitment consultants.

There were so many job ads for recruitment consultants. "What are they recruiting for?", I wondered. There are no jobs to be had. Fortunately, through my university jobs' board, I found an ad for something called the 'Pearson Diversity Scheme'. It was a summer programme that gave underrepresented groups an opportunity to be interviewed at businesses within the Pearson group. Companies like Penguin and - to my excitement - The Financial Times. I applied, completed the rounds of interviews, and found myself with a paid summer internship on the editorial team at the FT, rotating around different desks.

Working at the FT as my first post-graduation job was an amazing opportunity to learn how the best minds in the world get things done. I was thrown into the deep end which was a good thing - it encouraged me to be an attentive listener and take initiative. The idea of being a writer had always appealed to me because since a baby I was a sucker for stories. As a child I had a vivid imagination and would write fantastical fairy tales complete with illustrations. To my mother's frustration my original canvas was the white wall behind her sofa. Eventually I was given stationary of my own and would scribble away. I always had a journal which I'd fill with poems, plot ideas and characters. As I got older I decided to invest in a typewriter that I stumbled across in a jumble sale in order to cement my writer's credentials. You have to look the part, right?

This love of storytelling didn't stop at writing poems and stories, it extended into acting and performance. As a kid I was captivated by the stage. I loved the idea of becoming someone else and telling their story in a believable way. As a result I did a lot of acting as I grew up. I would audition for every school play and even joined the drama society at LSE and acted in a play in my first term at university. Telling stories, making stories, being stories - I'd spent all my life doing it and I enjoyed it. I believe these experiences have helped me become the confident public speaker I am today.

While studying at LSE I started taking my writing more seriously and was interviewed to become the Style Editor of the student union's newspaper. After a successful year of that, I decided to put myself forward for Editor of the Arts section. In this post I not only contributed stories - I put ideas into fruition and inspired our team to seek out compelling narratives to make our paper fly off the shelves. I always enjoyed the act of spinning a yarn. I always felt it was more than just escapism but a real art, an effective way of communicating ideas clearly and drawing in your audience.

So it's odd that despite having this love for telling stories it took me so long to realise the importance of storytelling in the world of work. I always knew a writer needed to tell a story effectively to capture the audience's attention but I never drew the parallel with a job candidate and an employer. If a great story is what pulls you in and leaves you begging for more, why should great stories end on the stage or in the pages of what we read?

When I first started work I didn't have a narrative or clear direction of where I wanted to end up and as I result I didn't choose the jobs I went into - they chose me. After 7 years of letting serendipitous introductions and recruiter messages forge my career path, I realised it was time to tap into my storytelling powers for the betterment of my career. I wanted more leadership roles and more marketing experience, so I emphasized my relevant achievements as a leader and marketer. I had been accountable for significant growth targets and had achieved them. I realised that, when I really thought about it, I had lots of achievements to talk about. I could paint a picture with my achievements to show not only who I was, but who I could be if given the right opportunity.

This is what it's all about, being able to turn your collection of unique experiences and transform them into a story that makes you a perfect fit for the role. I meet lots of graduates who are studying a vocational subject like law but who are very interested in getting into startups. They often tell me that they're reluctant to apply for startup jobs because they feel that they aren't 'techie' enough or have no startup experience. The truth is, when you're a university student your real life work experiences are limited (unless you're in the minority / an outlier) and that's OK. Employers won't expect you to know the ins and outs of the job. They care about the transferable skills you possess, as well as other useful qualities like your ability to solve problems, your ability to work hard and your ability to work under pressure or to a deadline with a team.

From your experiences throughout school and life you will have countless examples of things you have achieved and accomplished. Your life is unique and full of interesting things - it's all about perspective. You know your life inside out but if you're anything like me or most of the people I meet in my workshops you don't think you have much to say about yourself. But by learning to turn your unique experiences into a story you can create an alluring and enticing perspective for future employers. In the case of my non-techie grads, I encouraged them to think about sports teams they played on at school, whether they were prefects or granted any other special roles or elected positions. I ask about prizes they may have won or any special projects they have participated in. All of these are hard-won achievements you should be proud of, and they contribute to the stories you tell to prospective employers.

Master CV:

I always recommend that everyone have a master CV. Your master CV is a living document that lists all of your experiences. Every single one. Top scores you achieved throughout school, prizes you won, sports teams you played on. It's literally a checklist of every single accomplishment you have to your name. It's a rolling roster of everything good you have done - from tasks you've completed during summer camps to plays you've performed in for your local church. You should create your master CV with no shred of judgement or critique. It should be exhaustive and hold nothing back.

Your master CV is your long list, a stream of consciousness, a free flow where you note every role and responsibility you've ever had. The space where the master CV lives is free from your usual judgements and your perfectionist formatting. It is where you simply list everything you've done and every achievement you've earned from school to now. If you really open your mind this should be a few pages long. This will form the basis of every new CV for a specific role. Can you remember your first ever CV? Maybe you wrote it in your teens. What did you cram into the bullet points which now give you writer's block? I bet your younger self had no qualms about dropping in little achievement bombs like "Selected to be a finalist in the spelling bee."

Remember that your CV is your future employer's first impression of you, your first opportunity to be memorable. Make this as effective as possible by drawing attention to your interesting range of responsibilities, your diverse skill set and your unique achievements. If you're still finding it tough to get the wheels in motion, approach building your master CV in a different mindset. Imagine you've been employed as a copywriter to look at another person's past experiences and achievements (at both school and work) in order to sell them to future employers. If this copywriter were to look through all your past achievements and experiences—what would they write?

It's important to find a way to feel positive and not awkward about promoting yourself. Remind yourself that you worked hard for those accolades. Every bullet point on your CV is a trophy you should show off proudly. These are assets that distinguish you from the competition, that get you through to the next stage of hiring. Quantify as many of your achievements as possible. This gives a measure to recruiters and helps them compare you more objectively with other applicants. It also forces you to be less vague and give more detail about work you've done in the past and the results that you achieved.

People often ask me "How much does design matter?" Based on my experience in hiring rounds, unless you're going for a purely creative role, very little. On the aesthetic front, what matters most is ease of reading, clear and consistent formatting, faultless grammar and no typos or spelling mistakes. Ensure you use simple formatting like bold and italics to draw the recruiter's attention to specific themes or highlights. They should only serve to break up text in order to make your CV easier to digest. They should be used consistently and sparingly and not be distracting.

Think of your CV as your billboard, sending signals to a future employer about your abilities. And what do you do when there's a gap between where you are now / what your experience says about you, and where you want to be? Bridge that gap in your opening summary. In a few short but powerful sentences, draw the reader in with the relevant buzzwords and big brand names that signal you have high quality experience, signing it all off with a few words on what you aspire to achieve next. Link the words in a way that makes its conclusion (i.e. your future aspiration/their open position) a logical next step. This is your elevator pitch, your rehearsed default answer to the 'tell me a little bit about yourself' phone-screen opener. Work on this as much as you need to. Draft it, re-draft it, test it out and reiterate. Eventually you'll land on something you like, something that rolls off the tongue and will stick.

Once you have your master CV locked and loaded, applying for different roles becomes a simple exercise of adapting the master CV into a tailored CV for each role, cross referencing the job description bullet points against your own long list of achievements. You'll be able to present an edited, curated list painting you as the perfect person for that open position. Your CV may be your one and only first impression, but it's just the first in a long list of tests you need to ace in order to land that dream job.

Creating the role-specific bespoke CV is a simple process of matching their requirements to your relevant accomplishments. Before creating a new copy of your master CV which you will edit down for the role, spend some time researching the company, the role and the team you're joining. Immerse yourself in the information you have available. Once you feel like you understand their brand, what motivates them, and what they're looking for in the role, you're ready to start creating your bespoke CV. I always encourage people to use a different CV to apply for each different role because you want to highlight the most relevant skills and achievements from your life depending on what the employer is looking for. Using your master CV, edit the less relevant parts out and expand on the more relevant sections. Ensure you're showing off the skills and experiences you have and which they are looking for.

Cover letters:

I am not a fan of cover letters. I appreciate that they are used as another screening tool for recruiters to distinguish between candidates, or even to narrow down the pile when job postings receive an influx of applications, but whenever I've been involved in recruitment I've never bothered to read them. I've witnessed many cover letters being ignored or discarded. I also know how annoying it is writing them, I remember from my own experiences how long it takes to draft them, and what a generally frustrating experience it is. Knowing that, and knowing how many are ignored, leaves me with a bad taste in my mouth when I think of them at all. That said, many companies still ask for cover letters or, at the very least, a short blurb about why you want to work for their company and why you think you are a good fit for the role.

All good cover letters I have seen and which I have written that have landed me interviews are concise and show that I have researched the company and the role. They have expanded on elements of my CV in greater detail, specifically the experiences which are most closely related to the role I am applying for. Ideally, the first lines of your cover letter will open with a summary of your experiences (e.g. your headline, which we will cover in the next chapter) and a positive declaration about the company/role and why you want to work there. I recommend going to the company website or blog to see what their latest announcements have been, and also checking online news stories to see what positive stories have been covered in the press. Reference these data points in your cover letter.

Your cover letter should be no longer than one side of paper and be as structured as possible. A simple structure that has worked for me is:

- Powerful opening line introducing myself and my reasons for wanting the job/why I think I will excel in it.

- First paragraph going into more detail than my CV about the specific skills I have that make me suited.

- Second paragraph elaborating on a specific experience/project I worked on that correlates closely with the responsibilities of the job.

- A third paragraph elaborating on the company mission and values and why it is the only place I would like to work.

Dream Big. Hustle Hard.

- A closing line clarifying my availability for follow up questions and interview and my contact details.

Like all things application-related, ask a friend or relative to review your work for typos before you submit.

tl;dr

- Create a master CV that is a no-holds-barred list of all your achievements throughout your school life and your extracurricular activities. If you're kind to yourself, as you should be, this should be many pages long. Keep this document regularly updated.

- Use your master CV as a starting point to develop tailored CVs for every job application. Tailor it according to the job description to suit the specific role. Cut out the irrelevant sections and expand on relevant ones.

- Put yourself in the recruiter/hiring manager's shoes and think about what skills they have asked for in the job description. Select points from your Master CV which best illustrate how you possess these skills.

- Quantify your achievements as much as possible to give them context and a point of comparison to your peer group e.g. "achieved highest Chemistry grade in school year of 600 students" sounds more impressive than "achieved highest Chemistry grade in school year" People can be cynical and they might suspect the latter is a small sample size in a small school.

Chapter 10
How to prepare for interviews so you maximise your offers

- You can never do too much research or be over prepared when it comes to interviews.

- Approach the interview like you are pitching yourself for the role and sell yourself.

- Use the STAR method to answer competency questions and give your responses structure.

- Ask questions which show you can think strategically about the business and take the role seriously.

One evening while I was still studying at LSE I found myself in the Three Tuns, our student union bar. I was hanging out with my friend and his boyfriend moaning about workload and employment prospects as most final year students do. My friend turned to me and said, "Surely you've got some interviews lined up?" to which I answered, "I do, in fact I have one tomorrow." He glanced at me in surprise. "So you have a job interview tomorrow and you're here in the pub with me?" The penny dropped and I made a swift exit, rushing home to cram in some prep. Needless to say, I didn't get the offer. There are some lessons you have to learn the hard way. But what I learned from that experience is that you can never be too prepared and, most of the time, the amount of effort you put into something determines the results you achieve in the end. The technique outlined in this chapter has served me so well since I have committed to it that I wished I had been doing this all of my career. In the space of a month of preparing in this way, I turned six interviews into six offers and was able to play them against each other to earn myself the best compensation (more on negotiating in the last chapter.)

I've learned that it's most effective to treat preparing for an interview like a research project, a dissertation or thesis. This detailed research and effort isn't only meant to give you the best possible chance of getting the job, it's also an opportunity for you as a prospective employee to do your due diligence and really be sure that the company is right for you. You want to be sure that your expectations of the company are affirmed by the data you have available. In the digital age it's very easy to find out exactly what you need to know to ensure that your interview goes smoothly and you're prepared for every question they can throw at you - even the surprise ones.

Interview research and preparation can be divided into the following sections:
- The company in the news: latest trends.

  ○ Go on Google News or relevant trade publications to see what's being said about the company, and understand the latest trends in the industry and what's affecting their market.

- Researching the interviewer(s).

  ○ Find their social media profiles e.g. LinkedIn, Twitter and Instagram to collect data points you can bring into small talk (and show off just how keen you are to get the job, you've done detailed preparation to help your case).

- Preparing examples based on the job description.

- Anticipating macro (high-level market /industry angle) or surprise questions.

- Practicing stalling tactics to help remain calm under pressure.

- Preparing sensible questions to ask at the end.

Now as someone who tends to shoot from the hip, I've had to force myself to develop frameworks and processes to fight against my instincts and really focus, concentrate and not overlook details. If you're like me, you might be sighing at the list above and thinking that this tedious work is not worth it. Well - it is. The job world is competitive. Why bother showing up to the interview if you can't be bothered to put in the preparation? You may as well not turn up because you're already accepting defeat if you decide to not maximise your preparation efforts and leave no stone unturned. If you really want something in a competitive job market you have to fight for it. And given we spend most of our waking lives at works it makes sense to fight for those job opportunities that we are most excited about. So, let's go through the list and tackle these preparation tips.

The company in the news: latest trends

Starting off by researching the company in the news helps you make relevant small talk at the start of the interview as you may have to walk with your interviewer from the lobby to the meeting room. After pleasantries are exchanged, it could set you apart from other candidates to remark upon a news story relating to the company e.g. a new product release or international acquisition. This also gives you some fodder for when they inevitably ask why you want to work for the company. It's a question that almost always comes up. It's likely that you would have already answered it in your cover letter if you had to write one. Let's say one of the reasons you want to work for the company is that they are the most innovative maker of X. If they have just released a new version of X in the week of your interview and you were the first person in your social circle to get your hands on it, you could bring this up as a further example of why they are the company for you.

Researching the interviewer(s)

I also like to research the interviewer before I go to interviews. Most companies will let you know who will be conducting your interview. For example, the job description for a Marketing Executive role at Agency Z might say "Reporting into the Director of Marketing….", which means you should Google "Agency Z Director of Marketing" and see what you can find. Have they done any interviews recently? If so, what did they say? Are they commenting on trends that affect their industry? You might have a chance to reference their opinion when you finally meet. Also check out their LinkedIn profile. Does anything interesting stand out about their previous roles within the organisation, or their past employers? You might notice that before they joined the marketing team they started out in the product team, and that might lead you to ask how their experience within the product team impacts their marketing strategy. That's the kind of question that will make you memorable if no other candidates took the time to research the interviewer's background. You may even find that they attended the same university as you, or used to live in a city abroad where you've visited on holiday. All of these facts create talking points you can work into the conversation to show how interested you are in the team and also how committed you are to getting the role.

Matching real life examples to the job description:

The next step is really the most important. It's all about creating relevant examples for each bullet point in the job description. To really understand why this matters it's helpful to put yourself in the shoes of the hiring manager/interviewer. Remember that the interview is just like a sales pitch. The interviewer has lots of different people to choose from for the role - but you want her to choose you. To put yourself in the best position to be picked remember what the interviewer is looking for. They've put all their requirements in the job description, so the person who best fits the job description is the person they will want to hire.

Re-read the job description a few times when you're preparing, perhaps print it out along with a copy of the CV you sent them (the hiring manager is likely to have this in front of them when they chat to you). The next step is to create examples from roles on your CV that demonstrate each bullet point requirement. When I do this I use my notebook, one which fits in my bag, so I can keep cramming my notes when I'm en route to the interview. I find the best way to prepare is to write one of the job description bullet points at the top of the page, and underneath that bullet point, write an example from past work experiences which illustrates the required skill.

I recommend writing your examples in the STAR structure:
Situation
Task
Action
Result

This is the best way to respond to competency questions i.e. the questions which typically start "give me an example of a time when you..." and is a helpful way to prepare examples in general because it gives you a clear structure with which to explain past scenarios. It's logical and efficient and has helped me win many offers. Remember that most interviewers complete interview notes on each candidate. The more detailed, structured and clear your responses are, the easier it will be for the interviewer to catch the relevant data points which show that you meet the requirements of the job. Clear and structured responses also give you a competitive advantage over the other candidates.

The STAR structure enables you to give an example in a concise way, which is really helpful for chatty people like me who tend to drag out stories and include unnecessary details and go off on rambling tangents. The STAR structure starts by laying out the 'situation'. This is the sentence which sets the scene, painting the picture for what is to come next. An example I have used in the past is "The summer after my A-levels I worked as a street fundraiser for the charity Amnesty International." The next step is the 'task'. This is ideally a problem which you had to solve and one which you solved successfully. Using the same example I would say, "I was tasked with signing up eight new customers before the end of the day to hit my target and earn the maximum commission".

Next comes the 'action' i.e. what you did to solve the problem. "I made sure that I greeted every single person that passed me on the street and if they stopped to chat, I gave them a really detailed pitch about how even the smallest donation could help rehabilitate child soldiers. I reminded people that the minimum donations started at just £4 a month and could be cancelled anytime, as most objections relate to the donations amount and being tied into a direct debit for ages". The 'result' is literally that - the outcome or what happened. It should always relate back to the 'task' i.e. problem and clearly show how you resolved it. Using the same example I would say "I was able to sign up 8 people by 5pm and a 9th person before my shift ended at

6pm, beating my record, getting the most sign-ups on my team that day and earning the highest commission I ever had." Try to quantify the result as much as you can to add context and make it more concrete.

As you're preparing your examples ahead of the interview, try to focus on examples which do end with a positive result. The examples are your opportunity to show off about your skills and remember this is your chance to separate yourself from the competition. Don't hold back and don't be shy. Interviewers can't read your mind and really wanting the job isn't enough to get it. You need to be explicit and give all the information you can to show how you're the best person for the job. Most of the companies I've worked for in the past, and this is particularly true of startups, want candidates to demonstrate leadership skills. They want individuals who can take the initiative and be assertive when it comes to finding solutions. This means being confident in your abilities and being able to sell yourself as the ideal candidate.

Be sure to pick examples that demonstrate your leadership skills and put you at the centre of the problem you are solving. You may have to amplify your involvement to make this happen but that's OK, everyone does it. This is your time to shine, your time to try and get the job you really want. The difference between you and an identical candidate getting an offer for the job could come right down to who is better at selling themselves.

To ensure all bases are covered, it would be worth preparing a couple of examples that illustrate when something went wrong at work, or when you had a disagreement with a team mate and how you resolved it. Most jobs will require an element of teamwork and problem solving and, above all, no company wants to hire someone who is just plain mean. So be prepared to be asked a question relating to a negative experience at work and be sure to present your response in a way which paints you in a positive light despite the negative experience. A common example I heard when interviewing recent graduates related to group projects at university where one team member was not pulling their weight on a project. In many examples the interviewee would explain how they took the individual to one side to try to understand the lack of motivation and flexed their interpersonal skills to reach a resolution that worked for the team. Perhaps you have a similar example from school, university or a sport you play.

What if you're struggling to think of examples?

This is why having a master CV on file is really helpful. If you're struggling to think of examples it's probably because you are trying to think of perfect examples from the last few months. If you're just starting out on your career you're not likely to have many real life work examples. If so, use examples from school. Did you work on any independent study projects like an extended essay? Were you on any sports teams? Were you a prefect? What accomplishments and achievements do you have from school that you can use to show off your skills and qualities? Don't worry too much about trying to find a perfect example or an accomplishment which seems extraordinary or exceptional. The important thing is to have an example which simply demonstrates you have the specific skill.

If you're still struggling to put together a good STAR example, it may be because you've picked too complex a 'task'/problem. When I've taught this tactic in workshops at universities, I've noticed that the students who would tell me that they were struggling had usually picked a problem which was really too big. A problem which was actually lots of separate problems compounded into one. Sometimes you can take an example from the past and pick it apart so that it actually has more than one 'task' or problem that you solved using different skills. The simpler and more straightforward the 'task'/ problem, the better. It will make it easier for you to explain and make it easier for the interviewer to understand.

What to remember:

- Interviewers have to make offer decisions based only on the information you give them, so don't hold back and be sure to get all your great attributes and passion for the role into the interview.

- Interviewers rarely try to trip you up on purpose. If you sense negative energy just remember that the interviewer might be having a bad day for a whole multitude of reasons. Don't take it personally or let their energy impact yours. Keep your eyes on the prize, stay focused and professional.

- The questions you ask are just as important as the questions you answer. The end of the interview is the perfect time to show off how well you have prepared if you haven't already had the chance to do so. It's another opportunity to set yourself apart from the competition.

How to answer tricky questions:

In workshops at universities I'm often asked how to field these commonly asked but tricky questions. While I don't encourage dishonesty I do think it's fair not to be fully transparent all the time. In the complex changing landscape of the employee-employer relationship, no one really is. It's important to remind yourself in those challenging moments that the job market is exactly that - a marketplace. You are competing against other candidates for the job. Therefore the onus is on you to do everything reasonable to maximise your potential for getting an offer.

Similarly, think about how no company ever says negative things about their culture or the work experience on their company website or in their communications with you. Companies are doing their best at every moment of the recruitment process to hide any negative aspects about them that might put you off the job. Now, if every company is as perfect as they say they are, why do employees quit? Why are employees unhappy? Why do some people feel they could be paid more? Or work less? There is an asymmetry of information going on and it is in the employer's benefit to keep it that way. A great example of this is how salaries are hidden. Wouldn't it be great to know what everyone who does the role you are applying for is paid? Of course it would! For you. But not the company. If the company can get you to do the same job for the absolute minimum, which could mean you are earning less than people in the same role who negotiated harder or whatever, they will. It will save them money. My tactics are all about helping you as a jobseeker get onto a more level playing field with the potential employer.

Here are some common tricky questions and my suggestions on how to respond:

"What's your salary expectation?"

Go online to research what the median salary is for the job title you are going for. Websites like prospects.ac.uk often publish this data. Glassdoor also publishes data given by past employees but you can't guarantee its accuracy. Frame your answer according to the 'market rate for the role based on your years of experience' and remember that compensation is about more than just your salary. You will also want to take into account the full range of benefits - pension, private healthcare, total annual holidays, work from home options. You should already have in your mind what an ideal compensation package would look like and be ready to state this explicitly when asked.

"Are you interviewing with any other firms / have you received any other offers?"

Think of what this question is really asking. It's asking, "Are other companies interested in you? Are our competitors interested in you? How desirable are you as a candidate?" Even if you have not heard back from your pending applications, assume that you will and say yes. Do not say who the companies are - you don't have to do that. And if you haven't actually received an offer yet you risk the recruiter contacting someone there to double check. I've answered this question in ambiguous ways e.g. "yes another big US tech firm has made me an offer, but I much prefer your company". Be sure that however you answer this question, you make it clear that your preference is for their company. To maximise your total number of offers, you should say that to every company that asks you. Don't hate the player, hate the game.

Macro questions about the industry:

It's possible you could be asked questions about the industry, or perhaps even about how ongoing current affairs might impact the industry. Just be sure you have brushed up on the news, and particularly the industry news, so you have a picture of what is going on. I like to think of it as 'the CEO perspective'. When the CEO of the company opens his news app or newspaper the morning of your interview - what are some of the things that might concern him? Has a competitor just launched a new product that threatens their product? Has legislation been passed by the government that will threaten their profits? If you really want the job you will be happy to invest time looking into the overall market landscape. Doing this extra bit of research also gives you some great questions that you could ask at the end of the interview.

Sensible questions to ask at the end:

As mentioned, if you haven't been asked any high-level questions about the industry, you could use the time at the end to ask how certain changes might be impacting the company's strategy going forward. This signals that you've been doing your research, but also shows that you can think about the company from a leadership perspective. I also like when individuals have asked me questions relating to my personal experiences of what it's like to work there - questions which can't be answered by reading the company blog e.g.

- What's changed the most in the time you have worked here?

- How does this company compare to your previous employer X (again, showing off that you've researched the interviewer)?

- How do all the different departments interact and communicate with each other to ensure things keep running smoothly?

And if the person interviewing you is who you are reporting to, you could ask one of my all-time favourite questions:

- What is your leadership style?

As a woman in a male-dominated field it has become increasingly important for me to ask questions related to diversity and inclusion. My happiest office environments have been the ones in which there is a great range of diversity across age, gender, race, religion, musical tastes, hair colour, economic background, sexuality…. The list goes on. As such, other questions I have asked (which still got me offers!) include:

- What percentage of your staff are women? (especially as many privately held startups and tech companies don't have to publish this information)

- What steps are you taking to make the team more diverse?

- What steps are you taking to make the workplace more inclusive? How successful have you been so far?

Stalling tactics / buying time / conquering nerves:

Even the most prepared candidates can be caught off guard. It's happened to me on many occasions but these tactics have helped me persevere. If asked a question I can't answer straight away, I will respond saying, "That's a really good question." In fact, I will likely pause - look pensive - then say "Oh, that's a really good question" drawing out each word slowly - but not suspiciously so - giving myself more time to think of a good answer. Sometimes I will ask them to re-phrase the question by saying something like, "Oh that's a good question. Do you mean in the context of [insert relevant point here]?" If it's a question where I know some of the answer but not all of it, I might say, "Based on my understanding of [insert whatever it is |, I think...". This would be to show them how my mind is working, and what the rationale/logic for my answer is based on. If I have no clue what the answer is, I will be honest and say, "I don't know but I do know... x,y,z" bringing in some other piece of information I know related to the subject.

Often tricky questions are used in an interview to test how you handle stress. In the startup world particularly, the ability to work with ambiguity is highly valued. But working with ambiguity is something we never do at school or university. In academia there is a syllabus and we stick to it. In startups and many other workplaces priorities are in flux and constantly changing. So it is important that employees can be stoic about unpleasant surprises and keep moving forward.

Be mindful of your breathing, body language and eye contact during the interview process. Pace your breathing so that, in turn, your speech is paced at an even rate. You don't want to speak so quickly the interviewer struggles to hear you. You also don't want to mumble. I recommend that you practise some of your STAR examples in the mirror to help you build confidence, train your voice and to see what you look like when you're answering the questions.

Make sure you're given a glass of water at the start so you don't end up choking on your dry, nervous throat at any point during the interview. Sit leaning forward with your arms or elbows on the table. It's important to lean in as it subconsciously sends the message that you are engaged and present, as opposed to leaning back with your hands in your lap suggesting you are passive.

Go on the company website to understand more about the dress code. At most tech companies and startups casual wear is fine, but it doesn't hurt to be smart. Wearing smart clothes will help you get into a serious mindset to deliver a winning interview. Be sure to bring a notebook and pen with you into the interview so you can take note of any interesting points mentioned. Ideally it will be the notebook you've been using to prepare so that, while you are commuting to the interview, you can get in some extra revision.

Give yourself plenty of time before the interview to arrive near the location well in advance. Ideally with enough time to sit in a cafe nearby and gather your nerves. Be sure you are at the office at least 15 minutes before your scheduled interview time. If you have never been to the offices before you should spend the night before your interview planning your route, planning your outfit and then get a good night's sleep.

During the interview be the best version of yourself. Even though you will be nervous and talking to a stranger, try to imagine you are opposite your favourite teacher or lecturer or relative. Someone who you respect and admire but can also have a laugh with. Send out your authentic positive energy so the person on the other side of the table walks away thinking - I would really like to have her on my team. She knows her stuff and seems really nice.

Activity:
- If you have an interview coming up, bring up the job description for the role on your laptop or phone.

- Write each bullet point of the job description at the top of a page of your notebook.

- For each bullet point, write an example underneath in the STAR structure.

    ○ Situation:
    ○ Task:
    ○ Action:
    ○ Result:

- Now practice reciting the examples in your mirror without using your notes, practicing the examples out loud will make you feel more confident in the interview.

Framework:

This is the longest chapter of the book because it is the most important. I've run countless workshops at universities like Oxford, LSE and UCL all about mastering the interview. The key takeaways are that the interview process is a two-way street where the cards are not all on the table. I like to think of it like a game as there are certain moves both you and the employer can play. The better you are at anticipating the employer's moves, the more likely you are to win. Get into their head and do what you can to convince them that you are the person they want. The more you can research and immerse yourself in everything there is to know about them, the easier it will be to assimilate so that by the time you meet face to face it's like you're already a part of the team. Confidence isn't something we are born with - it is something which is nurtured through practice and reward and grows over time. So rehearsing in the mirror, or with friends, will help you grow your confidence.

tl;dr

- Treat the interview like an exam. Take notes about the company and the role, prepare your responses and revise them.

- Prepare sensible questions to ask at the end that show you've done your research and touch on issues which matter to you about the workplace.

- The night before ensure you have researched how to get to the office and plan your journey in advance so you have plenty of time to get there.

- Plan your outfit the night before and get a good night's sleep so you can wake up stress free and ready to rock.

- Maintain eye contact with the interviewer, give off an authentic positive energy and lean in, with elbows or hands on the table, signalling your leadership capabilities.

PART III: NEGOTIATING OFFERS AND GRADUATING FROM GRIT CAMP

Chapter 11
Employers: Spotting red flags and negotiating offers

- Recruitment is a two-way street and you never have more power and influence in the employee-employer relationship than when you are a prospective candidate with an offer on the table.

- Understand what kind of job and environment will help you thrive and use the interview process to get relevant data.

- Never ever accept the first offer - negotiate for more of one of your priorities e.g. pay, training, holidays, flexibility etc.

It took me a couple of years working in the real world to come to the realisation that a working relationship is exactly that - a relationship, a union of two parties, something in which both sides will have to compromise at some point in time. At the beginning of my career I always felt like the employers had all the power. I felt like the prospective employer had me by the proverbial balls, and as a desperate jobseeker I should just make myself as compliant as possible to get the job. This meant that in my very first permanent graduate job, I soon became incredibly unhappy. There was a manager in the office who I felt had a personal vendetta against me, often criticising me in public and ridiculing me one on one. It was torture. I learnt from that experience to pay a lot more attention to who my manager would be in future job-interview situations.

How can you spot the red flags when you're job hunting to save yourself miserable moments at work? It's important to start by thinking about what is important to you. One thing that's become more important to me as I've got older is having lots of diverse people on the team. I find that being the only woman or only non-white person or only multicultural person in a corporate environment can be quite isolating, particularly when you want to speak up. I've had situations at work where I've tried to make a valid point, or object to a specific suggestion, only to have my feedback dismissed as 'emotional', after a male colleague's trivial objections were acknowledged without a blink. Think about what kind of work environment will enable you to thrive - write a list of the ideal qualities you want your co-workers to have and what kind of work culture you would like to see. Use the interviews to ask about this, but also remember that your employers are trying to pitch to you, too and don't have it in their best interests to be transparent. That's where websites like Glassdoor, which I mentioned earlier, come into play as well as informal conversations with entry-level employees in the business and those who have left. Use your networks and social media to do due diligence and find out what it's really like to work there.

Also remember that actions speak louder than words. What can you learn about the prospective employer from how they are behaving towards you. Are they great at communicating? Giving clear instructions about the recruitment process, the next steps, and being responsive to your questions? Or do they come across as a bit scatty and disorganised? Remember, employers typically put on their best behaviour to attract prospective employees. So if you are sensing anything fishy now, or picking up any signals that they aren't very attentive, very organised or very nice, it's likely to be a far worse situation behind the scenes.

The same goes for how you're treated in the interview. Yes, people can have bad days. But more often than not the people who are 'off' with you in an interview are a red flag. It indicates the attitudes that are accepted in that workplace. You might bring up the issue with a recruiter only to be told, "they were 'having a bad day' and they're not usually like that, trust me" - but be wary. It could be a line HR uses all the time, and they might just always be like that. Remember, interviews are a two-way thing. Not only are you trying to convince the company that you're the right fit for them, they should also be trying to convince you that they are right for you. Again, I've learned this the hard way and know many friends who have been in similar boats with prickly people in interviews who end up being just as prickly if not worse when they start working with them. Pick up on these signals, make a note of them, and bear them in mind as you make your decision about which job to accept.

How emotionally intelligent are the people interviewing you? How do they respond when you ask a follow-up question or ask them to repeat something that you don't understand? Are they patient? Are they letting you finish your train of thought and finish explaining your ideas? Or are they interrupting you? Are they coming across as cold or uninterested? As women, we typically perform higher on the emotional intelligence index than men and tend to have more empathy (forgive my sweeping generalisations). In the workplace, this isn't always a good thing. If you pick up on the emotions of others more easily you might be adversely affected by a co-worker who is very blunt or a co-worker whose emotional intelligence doesn't quite match up to yours and so quite often ends up rubbing you the wrong way unintentionally. Remember - this is your life, your career, your path to fulfilment and success. You need to be in an environment that empowers you and enables you to perform to your best abilities. Be sure you are picking wisely because it's a lot easier to turn down an offer than it is to quit a job.

There's a mindset called the scarcity principle which makes us place a higher value on the job we have than possible jobs we could have if we quit. It's this principle that makes talented but unhappy people stay in jobs they hate even when recruiters approach them on LinkedIn all the time. Because of this it's important to really look for the red flags while you're still in the recruitment phase. You should aim to have at least three offers to pick from so you don't just pick the only one you are given. Remember the work you've put into your ideal jobs, your motivations and your priorities - these are the ideas that should guide your decision. Not desperation. Not scarcity.

The people you surround yourself with in your career play an integral part in the speed your career will take off. If you have supportive line managers and colleagues who nurture your growth and enable you to thrive, you will have a speedy trajectory. If you end up in a toxic environment, it will impact your ego and self-worth and could set you back a bit, as you will need time to recover from the ordeal, to reflect on the experiences and regain your self-confidence. Always remember to make decisions based on which roles best match your priorities and motivations. Avoid making decisions which are too reactive e.g. my last boss was a mean old woman so as long as my next boss is a nice young man I'll be fine. Wrong. If only the job world could be simplified in such a way. Your job satisfaction will depend on a number of variables like your job, your commute, your compensation, your training opportunities, your colleagues, your workload, your progression opportunities etc. It's far more rational to make decisions based on the opportunities which maximise your top priorities most.

We have a tendency to oversimplify to help us make decisions and help us feel more reasoned in how we approach things. My aim is to encourage you to fight some of your instinctive oversimplifications and approach the job hunt like a research project, so you can make a data driven informed decision that will serve you well in the long run. Of course, you can't mitigate every risk and you must accept that no job is perfect and that there will always be things you can't control. Even if it turns out that the ideal job you picked isn't what you expected - that's OK. Use the frameworks and activities in this book to decide your next best step. You always have a choice. This is your life, not your boss's, not your family's, not your partner's, not your friends. Your one-way ticket to your final breath. Your decision what to do with it.

Negotiating offers - never, ever settle:

It was while working at The Financial Times that I became obsessed with job hacks. They are shortcuts and rules that really successful people in the corporate world know all about and leverage. Tips and tricks many others are totally oblivious to. I suppose it was writing about money all day that made me start to wonder what the secrets were of those who really had it. A lot of it. Suddenly the saying "knowledge is power" took on a whole other meaning. In my simplistic academic-oriented way of thinking I always thought that meant being smart, or rather intelligent. But when news of Bernie Madoff's Ponzi scheme broke along with the credit crunch in general and the total discrediting of supposed 'smart bankers' who were really just crooks, I suddenly thought - wait a minute. Everyone's just hustling in some way really aren't they? I became obsessed with finding out smart ways to hustle - nothing untoward or illegal, but just tips and tricks which I could apply to my life, particularly my career, to be more successful.

It was in this vein that I first learned how to negotiate offers. My time at the FT had drawn to a close - it was a three month contract in Editorial that hadn't been extended. I wasn't too cut up about it but I was pretty gutted to return to my part-time university job in retail. Not that I didn't like the job, I just felt demotivated. Were all my three years slogging away at LSE for this? Selling womenswear in a department store – a role where I didn't need to use my degree? I started wondering whether my student loan debt was worth it.

It was at this point I coined a vulgar but effective phrase to describe my job hunt - I was whoring my CV out to the internet. Being the recession, I was open to anything. Through a lovely recruiter I eventually had an offer for a permanent job in a financial publishing company. I happened to be at the pub over the weekend when the email from the recruiter came through on my Blackberry. I was thrilled. I made a note to research 'negotiating offers' online when I realised that one of the guys sitting with us in the pub was a recruiter himself. I began my investigative research immediately and asked, "If you had a candidate who just got an offer, what could she say to make you fight for more money?" His answer was a simple formula which has never failed me since (often because it was true, although at this point in time it wasn't). He said, "Tell the recruiter that you're really excited about the offer because you love the company and the role, but you've also been offered a similar role by a similar company, who you don't like as much but are paying you more." He said that whenever that happens he wants to fight for the candidate to get the company they want to work with more and avoid them going to a competitor. Plus knowing that they are wanted by competition makes the prospective company want them even more. Try this next time you are given an initial offer as an extra bargaining chip. Hopefully, you will have followed my advice and actually have a number of real offers you can play against each other to maximise your earnings.

It is extremely important to note that salary growth happens a lot slower once you are in a company and nothing is guaranteed unless it's in a legally binding document. If in your negotiation process you are told that there will be an opportunity to increase your pay after X months - respond that that is an unacceptable term. I have had so many friends who were told this only for the promise never to materialise. When they try to bring it up with their managers or HR, they are told that circumstances have changed etc.

Remember, once you sign the contract, all bargaining power is lost. So never settle - negotiate for the terms that will make you happy to work at that company for the time that you expect to. I know so many people who have gone three years or more with no pay rise, who probably should have negotiated more at the start and should have continued to do so every year.

Unless something is explicitly stated in the terms of your employment contract, it is likely never to materialise. Your relationship with the company is about business, not friendship. Don't fall into the trap of believing your employee-employer relationship is more than just a monetary transaction. A transaction of your time and effort in exchange for their money and benefits. I know it might sound scary to suddenly get all serious and official about this but you absolutely must protect your value and understand what is at stake. This is business and this is your life. You will spend more time in the office than you will with your lovers, friends and family so flex your negotiation skills to maximise your earnings.

Sometimes to make my point in a different way I have opted for the less aggressive angle, stating something like, "while I don't doubt your promise that my pay will be reviewed in time, I have found it to be the case that only the terms which are set out in the employment contract seem to come to fruition, so I don't feel comfortable making this decision on your word alone. As a woman, in a world where there are huge gender pay gaps, it's important for me to negotiate and be paid my worth. Statistically, women are known to negotiate less than men and be paid less than men for the same job so I want to do everything I can to maximise my salary potential."

There are so many ways to get better compensation than increasing your base figure, as I have mentioned before. You could ask for a starting bonus. If they offer you a starting bonus at the outset, great. But ask for your bonus to be added to your base salary instead. That way, instead of a one-off payment, you get a much more valuable higher salary every year. If you're offered equity in the company you could ask for more. With equity offers do your research online and with the recruiter to get an accurate reading of what your equity is worth in the current market value. What other perks do you value? Maybe you want extra paid holidays? Flexible working? A training allowance? A new laptop? Whatever it is - don't be shy to ask for it. They want you at your most productive and only you know the formula to make that happen, so push for what you want.

Never underestimate the power of likeability. You can negotiate like a badass while still remaining extremely likeable. The person making the offer has found themselves at the negotiating table many times before. Do not feel bad for them, they would likely do the same in your position. If you've done your research about the market value for the role then you should be discussing sensible figures which they can't balk at. If someone reacts negatively to your negotiation attempts, that is a huge red flag. It's true that there are certain situations where men come off as 'domineering' while women using the exact same words and body language will be dismissed as 'aggressive' or 'bitchy'. If you sense that your negotiation efforts are being treated in a negative or patriarchal way, or worse still, if your offer is rescinded - thank yourself for pushing them to the limit and dodging a bullet. You could have been entering an environment in which strong women are derided instead of admired. That's a very dangerous and depressing place to start your career.

I've always enjoyed getting negotiation advice and practising negotiation tactics with my most accomplished male peers. Think of the most high flying working man you know and ask him about his last successful salary negotiation. Gain an understanding of what has worked for others, too. Then put together your own negotiating strategy which might be a combination of what I have suggested, what you have read online, what you have learned from friends and what feels comfortable to you. Whatever you do, don't avoid negotiating because it feels scary, you're satisfied with the first offer, or you're afraid of how it will make you look. None of those are good enough reasons to enter into a full-time job earning less than what you could have if you just opened your mouth. Not to motivate you through guilt but I do feel you owe it to the next generation of women who will also be demanding equality to start changing perceptions and making a case for your worth. The first offer you are given will be made on the lower end of the salary range because you are still early in your career and relatively junior. They also make an offer on the lower end of the range because they anticipate a negotiation. In my experiences of hiring I have never, ever, gone in at the upper limit of my budget, or with the highest offer. Remember, it is in the company's interest to hire you for as cheaply as possible. So do not be afraid to ask for more, whatever element that is, but absolutely do not settle. Do not perpetuate the reality where women are paid less than men simply because they don't ask for more.

Framework:

Read 'Ask for It' by Linda Babcock & Sara Laschever all about how women can use the power of negotiation to get what they want in the workplace. Think about how you can apply the lessons in our own life.

tl;dr

- Actions speak louder than words: what are you learning about the potential employer from the way they treat you during the recruitment process? Are they giving you the vibe that they will value you? Judge them by their actions not their words.

- Never settle. Don't put appeasing others / avoiding awkwardness before your right to earn. Always negotiate for something more. Employers expect

Dream Big. Hustle Hard.

this even if they give off the vibe it's unwelcome (that's *their* negotiation tactic).

Chapter 12
Grit: How to Embrace Rejection

- Spend some time understanding yourself better specifically where your fear of rejection and failure comes from, by doing so you can begin to control it.

- Do things which push you out of your comfort zone, including the unpleasant and scary, to build your resilience.

- Do not let past failures or disappointments define you nor impact how you feel about yourself and the decisions you make today.

I would be lying if I said I was happy with the thickness of my skin. Although I'm now 29 and have had a few years to get used to rejection letters and awkward interview questions I don't have the answer to, it doesn't make the experience any more pleasant. That said, I am grateful that my skin has got somewhat thicker than when I first started out in this crazy world called work. Why is rejection so painful? And what's the best way to prepare for it? I've learned that it's all about how you approach outcomes and the mindset you apply to the situation. I'm slowly getting to the point where I care less about how negative words make me feel, and care more about what I can learn from them to improve myself for the future. My relationship with rejection starts in my childhood and by unpicking its roots and my obsession with perfection I've been able to liberate myself from my old mindset and in doing so become far more resilient than I ever was.

When I was younger, I saw the world through my parents' eyes. Specifically my dad's eyes because he was the boss of the house - the breadwinner, the one you had to speak to when you were in trouble. Classic Nigerian patriarch. My dad has what Dr Carol S Dweck would call a 'fixed' mindset. For him, school work and work in general was all about the end result - getting the top grade, getting the highest position. He is not a fan of the phrase 'life is about the journey not the destination.' For him, life is the destination, the journey is just what you have to get through to reach it. So as a child, schoolwork thrilled and terrified me in equal measure. The way I saw it I had to achieve top marks in all my school work or my life would be a complete and utter failure.

There was no middle ground in my father's eyes. It didn't matter how hard I had worked, or even how I had approached the work, the only relevant thing was the outcome. I would be judged by the outcome, the result, not my dedication or effort. As I've got older I've realised just how limiting this mindset is and have tried to adopt what Dr Carol S Dweck would call a 'growth mindset'. Instead of obsessing over outcomes and judging myself accordingly, I reflect on the whole experience. Did I work my hardest? Did I do my best in the time I had available? If so, then what is there to cry about. Let me learn from this experience to think about what I can improve for the next time.

Unfortunately, it took me 29 years to get to this point, and I hope that you are already there or will get to it soon. My dad's obsessions with grades rubbed off on me and took a long time to shake off. I remember when my family first moved to Tanzania. I had been going to an ordinary elementary school in Maryland, USA up to this point, but now attended the International School of Tanganyika. It was a school which followed the British curriculum and I soon started the school year in the third grade having finished the second grade before I moved from America. I aced every assignment I was given. My parents and my teacher were concerned that I wasn't being challenged enough. It was decided that I would skip a grade, so I soon found myself in a new class with a new teacher just a few months after moving to a new country. My dad can be arrogant at times and framed this as the natural evolution of his genius DNA manifesting itself in me. In hindsight, it probably should have been explained to me in better detail that I was skipping a grade to be challenged more, and get the best out of my education. But all I really heard was 'I'm a genius! I'm a genius! I'm a genius! It runs through my veins!" It did great things for my ego but only stoked my painful relationship with failure and rejection.

I became obsessed with success and good grades, because that's when I received the most praise. On some level I started to think that support from my father was conditional on me receiving good grades. It wasn't completely in my head. If I missed any marks or had any type of constructive feedback on my report cards, he would nitpick every single one, scrutinising my teacher's words and critique-ing my efforts. He would go on with his favourite saying "To whom much is given much is expected" and I would feel guilty for letting him down, for disappointing him, vowing never again to let one mark go. It might also be helpful to add at this point that my dad is not the most affectionate or emotive of guys. In the absence of dad hugs, I latched onto his nuggets of praise and became obsessed with winning them.

On reflection, it's no surprise that I had a complete existential crisis at LSE when I found myself struggling to complete my economics problem sets, let alone ace them. When your identity rests on your academic success - quite frankly you've got problems on the horizon. You can't base your identity on things you cannot control. And you cannot control your grades. You can work hard, you can revise until your eyelids can't stay open, but you will not be the person to mark the paper and write down that final grade.

And you have to learn to be OK with that. Same goes for job interviews. You can only control the things you can control, and the hiring manager's mind isn't one of those.

I started to suspect I needed a mindset change during the Christmas holidays of my final year at secondary school. My parents were living in Abuja, Nigeria at the time and I was spending some weeks there on a break from boarding school. Just a few months previously I had spent a week at Balliol College, Oxford University, interviewing for the Politics, Philosophy and Economics (PPE) course. This was the same course my dad did at the very same college. The experience was mortifying to say the least. In my practice interviews at school, our careers adviser gave me ridiculously easy and misguided questions. "They'll start off with something easy, asking you how your train journey was, for example, to make you feel more relaxed." Ha! Did they ever! My first interview, which took place the day after we'd sat a gruelling three hour exam, took place at the top of a tiny dark turret somewhere on the college grounds. It was raining and I was a nervous wreck. My whole academic life, i.e. my WHOLE life, had been leading up to this moment. Every report card, every exam, every A came down to this - my Oxford University interview. This was why my dad had pushed me so hard, had sent me to one of the best private schools in the UK, to get me into PPE at Oxford and walk in his footsteps. It was all on me now. I couldn't fuck this up.

And yet I did. First of all, as I stood waiting to be called in standing in the rain, I must have got lost in my thoughts because I never noticed the student who had interviewed before me leave. Their departure was my cue to go up. I did wonder why it was a few minutes past my scheduled time and no one had come to get me, so I started up the stairs just as a teaching assistant was coming down, "Abadesi?" he asked, "Yes that's me!" I answered, 'Hurry up, you're late.' he snapped. Oh dear, if I wasn't already nervous and scared I was certainly bricking it now. Up I climbed this narrow staircase feeling like I was in a deleted scene from Harry Potter when I finally arrived at a professor's study. I couldn't make up this stereotyped scene if I tried. Enter a darkened study, leather-bound books piled high on every surface you can see. It's dark, save for one antique lamp sending out a faint orange glow from a desk. Behind the lamp sits an old man with a blank sheet of paper in front of him and a few sheets of paper in his hand. I approach.

"Hello, my name is Abadesi Osunsade, it's a pleasure to meet you" extending my hand. "Do sit down," is his reply. I notice the papers he is holding are my UCAS form including my personal statement. No bother - I'm ready for the small talk. Except there isn't any. Barely looking up from the papers he scribbles an algebraic equation on the plain sheet of paper between us. "Draw a graph to represent this equation" Immediately my brain blanks and I panic - I don't even have a pen! "Excuse me, sir, but I don't have a pen" the teaching assistant I bumped into in the stairway emerges from the shadows of the doorway tutting and shoving me a pencil. If my heart wasn't racing before it's about to pound its way through my rib cage now. I take a few seconds to gather my thoughts, think and then sketch. I wait for a reaction, I am given nothing. I vow to assault my careers advisor in an act of revenge the minute I return to school.

"You mention in your personal statement that you're interested in the cross section of economics and politics", the professor starts again, "Yes!' I eagerly reply. If we're moving onto my personal statement I've got this next part down. I was quite proud of it, I'd even managed to name drop Marx - my favourite economist and philosopher at the time - and was ready to speak passionately about why I wanted to pursue PPE. "You also mention the oil industry and its impact in your country Nigeria", "Yes" I said again, now starting to wonder where this was going. Finally, he delivered his punch "What is the price of a barrel of Texas crude right now?" Oh shit oh shit, I thought, had I read to the end of this week's Economist magazine? I wondered. Why are their issues always so damn long! I cursed to myself and at their editorial team. I could remember what it was a few weeks ago... would that be good enough? I reminded myself that it wasn't only the answer that was important, but rather showing your reasoning and your working of the problem, so I began to explain how when I last checked it was priced at $40? (I can't remember now...) but since then uncertainty in the Middle East and other oil producing countries had caused the price to go up etc. There was no reaction from his deadpan face and a piece of me died. It was my first Oxford interview and I was already a fuck up. A failure. A whole life wasted. The rest of the interview is now a blur. I think for self-preservation my brain has wiped the memories.

I do recall walking out, running down the stairs, grabbing my mobile phone and calling my dad (not caring about the international charges) and bursting into tears. It's over, I thought, my life is over. My dad told me not to worry and that I still had my philosophy and politics interviews to make it up "The economics interviewer is always the tough one" he comforted me. And it's funny because at that point I felt like I didn't even want to study PPE at Balliol anymore. I thought - if that nasty old bully is going to be teaching me, I don't feel like I want to be a part of it. But I felt like my life existed only in how my parents valued it, according to their wishes for me, their plans for me.

So fast forward to the Christmas holidays, when the post arrives with a letter bearing the Oxford University logo. At church that week my dad had led a special prayer asking that I receive my acceptance. That day, as I held the letter in my hand praying silently and hoping for the best, my stepmother reminded me that it wasn't the end of the world if I didn't get in. And she was right. The letter showed that I had not been offered a place and despite all my fears, I was still breathing, we were all still alive and the Earth was still turning. Although I was extremely disappointed and felt depressed all that day, sulking in my room, I was surprised to wake up the next morning feeling a hint of relief. I was suddenly freed from the burden of following my dad's footsteps. I was always worried that my academic record might not live up to his ... I was also worried that he would expect me to get a Ph.D. as he did, which was something I didn't want to do.

A part of me was also really happy that I didn't have to turn down LSE anymore. As beautiful as Oxford was, there was something about living in London that really excited me. I could picture myself living in this iconic capital and getting up to all sorts of adventures. It was also really helpful that my stepmother was on my side supporting me. She reminded me that failures are a part of life and all that mattered was that I had done my best. She also helped me put it into perspective - I had applied to six of the UK's top universities and every one of them accepted me except one. Were things really so bad? With every day that passed after the rejection letter my positive emotions outweighed my negative ones. I had enjoyed my LSE Open Day experience far more than my Oxford interviews... so it could stand to reason that I would enjoy going to university there more, too. Yes, I'd disappointed my dad. But so what? He didn't disown me. I was still alive. Life resumed as normal. After this ordeal I started to grow up a little bit and develop my own way of thinking about success. As I've already covered in the book, my first year at LSE sobered me up a lot, too. Success isn't a shortcut to happiness, and failure doesn't have to mean being depressed.

It's important to be kind to yourself, to love yourself and be proud and be grateful for the good things you do have. It's important to understand that failures are lessons. And we only grow as individuals when we are pushed out of our comfort zone. In the last year I've started reading about the leaders I admire, listening to them speak in podcasts and finding famous quotes they have said online. Spend some time reading about failure from the perspective of people you admire, you will realise it goes hand in hand with success. You can't have one without the other. The greatest athletes learn from their defeats, the greatest business tycoons learn from the times they lost money. Don't let a fear of failure stop you from taking risks, or turn you into someone who quits too soon. Learn to welcome disappointments. Think about the last time you saw a baby in your family trying to take their first steps. When she inevitably stumbled after a few nervous steps, what did everyone around her say? "Don't bother getting up, you will never walk, you will never succeed!" Of course not, they probably clapped, beaming smiles, cooing "well done!" and encouraging her to try again. Be that kind to yourself when things go wrong. You are the brave one for trying, and you are still the brave one, regardless of the outcome. You can succeed again!

With every day I'm trying to be more stoic in how I approach life. The only guarantees in life are that there are no guarantees. There are far too many moving parts for anything to be perfectly predictable. Embrace the unexpected, be prepared for the sadness and suffering that is an inevitability. That way, you will become more resilient. This doesn't mean you have to be cynical - not at all. It just means that you hold a mindset which leaves you mentally prepared for whatever life may throw at you. I'm often asked at talks or workshop how to be more resilient. It's such a great question that I'm sure has many right answers, but I will share what works for me. Experiences that have made me more resilient all involve something negative. Disappointment. Anxiety. Sadness. Fear. In the moment, I was down in the dumps, but on reflection if it happens again I'm ready. And this time I'll do better. So if you want to be more resilient, do more things that scare you. What are the things you have always wanted to do, the things you see people you admire do, but you are scared to try? Find a friend who's up for it and take the plunge. By leaving your comfort zone you give yourself the space to grow. By doing things that scare you, you thicken your skin. Take rejection for what it is - words. Just words. They can't kill you. They won't change you for the worse. And turn those words into something positive by asking, "what can I learn from this? Is there a lesson for me here? How do I improve on the feedback I have been given?" You'll start to realise that rejection really isn't that bad. In fact most times if you let enough time pass, you might be grateful for it.

Next steps after you get a rejection from an interview:

Everyone has had an interview where they were sure they smashed it, only to receive a rejection. I know I've been there a fair few times! And while it sucks to receive a negative outcome after all the preparation you put in, don't dwell on it too much if you can. The best course of action following a rejection is to ask for feedback. Be honest to your contact in the company and say something like, "I would really appreciate as much specific feedback as you can give so that I can take it into consideration in future interviews." Most of the time people will be able to tell you where your strengths were and where your weaknesses were. It might even be that there was just a candidate who had more experience than you. There will always be some variables that you cannot influence or control. Just take notes and keep all this information in consideration as you continue your job hunt. You could record the feedback you receive in your notebook and think about ways to incorporate it into your personal development. Be mindful of that fact that not all feedback is created equal. If something doesn't sound right, seek advice from a mentor. You won't always get honest, accurate feedback, that's just the way it is. You can add all the interviewers you met as connections on LinkedIn, thanking them for their time. Don't feel awkward. Business is business. You never know what might happen in the future, you might apply for another role or they might become your client.

Activity:

Look back on the past year and the work you have done - whether in your job or academia. Think about an event that you may have classified as a failure - an event where you feel that you let yourself down and you're disappointed by the outcome. Now that time has passed, can you try to re-examine this event with fresh eyes and think about what valuable lesson you learnt from it? Did you learn that you underestimate how long it takes you to get certain types of tasks done? Did you learn that you need to invest more time in developing a certain skill? Did you learn that there are more effective ways to communicate with the people you are working with? It might help to sketch your thoughts as a mind map on a blank sheet of paper. The idea is to turn the disappointments from wholly negative experiences into something which you can find a positive in - a learning, a lesson, a new idea. It's just like the saying - every cloud has a silver lining.

Framework:

Read Mindset by Dr Carol S Dweck all about the differences between a growth mindset and a fixed mindset. Think about how you can apply the lessons in your own life.

tl;dr

- If you struggle with rejection, do some introspection to really understand why. Keeping a journal or meditation might help you find clarity on where the roots of your fear of failure are and help you break free from them. Counselling and therapy help, too.

- If you succeed, it might feel like you've done everything right, whereas if you fail, then you have an opportunity to learn something about yourself, to help you make yourself better and improve for the future. In this sense, failures are a win.

- If rejected after an interview, follow up immediately after and ask for feedback to help you with future interviews.

Still have unanswered questions? Email me on abadesi@hustlecrew.co

88206820R00073

Made in the USA
Middletown, DE
07 September 2018